The Journal of Meshach
When God and Life Disappoint

Jeffrey S. Crawford

HILLSIDE HOUSE
PUBLISHING

The Journal of Meshach: When God and Life Disappoint
Jeffrey S. Crawford
Hillside House Publishing

Published by Hillside House Publishing, Springdale, AR
Copyright © 2021 Jeffrey S. Crawford
All rights reserved.

Cover Design by Mille Cooper

Library of Congress Cataloging-in-Publication Data

Library of Congress Control Number: 2021931076
Jeffrey S. Crawford

The Journal of Meshach
ISBN: 978-1-7327596-4-0

Printed in the United States of America.

For Dad
The wisest man I know

A Word Before We Begin...

I am not a king and I am not a god. I am like most men on earth. Simple. Ordinary. Forgettable.

My name is Meshach.

I have known both kings and gods, and kings who thought they were gods. I have had the honor of friending men who were far from simple, anything but ordinary, and certainly impossible to forget.

My occupation: Court recorder for the king. Or kings, I should say, at this point in my life. I have a gift with words, I am told, and so I was commissioned at a young age to employ said gift in service to the king. So I wrote for the king but also wrote, unofficially, of course, for myself.

Now I am old. My life is approaching its end and the time of my last breath draws nigh. I can feel it in my bones. I too easily lose my balance when I rise. A new pain seems to reveal itself each morning. I am cold even when the weather is warm. I thank God for my blanket and for the stewards who keep my fire stoked. But my fingers are still nimble and my eyes sharp. I have spent my life writing and in recent days I have been reading much of what I have written, going back years. So many years now, that the words I read seem to describe the life of another man – certainly not me. Yet, there it is – ink on parchment – a testimony to a life that is perhaps more remarkable than I would give it credit.

And so now I feel compelled to write again. Maybe compile is a better term, or organize and edit. I would certainly not equate my written words with those of Holy Scripture, but I do feel there is something there...in the stories of my life that testify to the extraordinary nature of an ordinary life lived in the shadow of both gods and kings.

Consider this an invitation, dear reader. An invitation to peer through the looking glass of my life. Perhaps we will find common ground, you and me. For though the events offered heretofore occurred long ago – so, so long ago now – I have come to believe that we all walk on level ground before the one true and living God, whose fingerprints smudge the margins of each page you are about to read. Because no matter what generation one lives in, no matter what continent one calls home, no matter what language one may speak (oh, I could go on because there is no end to the ways in which we draw lines to separate ourselves from one another), in the end we are all human. We are all the same at the core of it. Of this I am convinced. Maybe I did not believe so in my past, but now, yes...we are all much more alike than we are different. I have lived too much life to believe otherwise.

But I get ahead of myself. I will be quiet now and let the story speak for itself. If you are ready to turn the page, then you have my permission to do so now....

-1-

The Babylonians have arrived in the land of Judah with brutal efficiency. I overheard my father reporting the news to King Jehoiakim.

"The Egyptians have been defeated at Carchemish." His hands slammed down onto the battle table covered by the map of Israel and the surrounding region. "Pharaoh Neco is no more. Now the Black Wind blows toward Jerusalem." He placed his thick index finger on the map and drew a line with it all the way to the Holy City.

It is not for me to be privy to such news, but my friend Azariah and I often find ourselves roaming the secret passageways of the royal palace. We are old enough now, having reached fifteen years of age, that no one questions us. Being members of the royal family helps as well. Most assume we are skipping our lessons for good reason, or feel it is just not worth the pains it might cause them to question us. Nevertheless, we use our station to our advantage.

The city has been buzzing with rumors and talk. I knew my father was meeting with the king's military advisors this morning, and as soon as he broke counsel with them he headed straight for the palace war room. Azariah and I took the shortcut through an old and little-used passageway. The tunnel ended in an opening behind a great tapestry in the war room. We were able to slip around it and stand behind a large stone pillar to observe the meeting between my father, the king, and his other most trusted advisors.

Rumors have persisted that the Babylonians are coming and there is fear in the city. It has been over one hundred years since the Northern Kingdom fell to the Assyrians – that's long enough that some forget that defeat is possible, but not so long that others don't point to it as a warning.

Yes, the Southern Kingdom - Judah herself - along with the Holy City of Jerusalem is vulnerable. Both my mother and father believe so. I've heard them talking as well. I have good ears and I've learned to pay attention to details.

"We needn't fear this Black Wind, Magnus." King Jehoiakim sat at the table, leaned back with his arms crossed in front of him. He wore a stubborn look on his face, dismissive of my father. "They are *only* Babylonians. From the land of Shinar of all places. Theirs is a cursed land, by Yahweh himself. The book of Moses declares it. You label them the Black Wind as if they are some unstoppable force. Have you forgotten who our God is? Yahweh will go before us and protect us," he flippantly declared.

I almost laughed out loud hearing King Jehoiakim's declaration of devotion. But I restrained myself so as to remain undetected. It is common knowledge throughout Judah that Jehoiakim pays no heed to the God of Abraham, Isaac, and Jacob. He does not offer sacrifices in the Temple and he observes none of the holy feasts or special days. My father says he worships the pagan gods of Egypt, although to say so publicly would be treason, even for a cousin of the king as he is.

"Egypt has fallen! Did you not hear?" My father declared with more force. The veins on his neck bulged, his face red. "We have no one to protect us now. The Babylonians are coming. Our scouts report that they are marching on us even now. Our borders have been breached. It is only a matter of time."

"Let them come, then!" Jehoiakim came to his feet. He had obviously been pushed too far. "Neco was a weak ruler of Egypt. It was time for him to fall. We have always survived, Magnus. Have you forgotten? We are God's chosen people. That is why we thrived under Neco, and if Neco is now gone we will thrive under this new Babylonian king. What is his name again?"

"Nebuchadnezzar."

"Yes, Nebuchadnezzar. We will thrive under him as well. Let him come. Let them all come. We will talk and we will dine. The tribute we sent to Neco of Egypt we can now send to Nebuchadnezzar of Babylon. All will be well, my cousin. Trust me." King Jehoiakim offered a stern smile and left the room. The meeting was over.

I could see my father's face as he looked at the other men left standing around the table. No one had said a word during the whole exchange and no one said a word now. The looks on their faces communicated clearly - the Black Wind was coming and the king's only response was, "Trust me."

But what does one do when one doesn't trust the king?

A private entry in the Journal of Mishael
Third day of Tammuz, the third year of the reign of King Jehoiakim of Judah

The first year of the reign of King Nebuchadnezzar of Babylon
605 B.C.

-2-

The Babylonians have laid siege to the Holy City.

Jerusalem is under the thumb of Nebuchadnezzar and all is not well. As my father warned, the Black Wind has swept into our land with an unholy vengeance. Several families escaped the city two weeks ago, choosing to flee to the green country of the north where the trees and smaller villages provide safety and protection. There are many places to hide in the north, my father says. His desire was for me, my mother, and my sister to join a local leatherworker who works just inside the Lion Gate, along with his family, and to make our own escape with them to Galilee. Father would stay, of course.

Sensing the exodus, King Jehoiakim declared that all members of the royal family must stay in Jerusalem. He even went as far as to place guards around the palace and family dwellings to ensure our compliance. The declaration came on the eve of our leaving and I doubt I will ever forget the look of disappointment on Father's face. It's as if he knows something I don't know. But I do know. I know what the Babylonians do when they take a land for their own. They rape. They burn. They pillage. And they take people – young people like myself – and they export them to the far reaches of their realm.

I don't believe my father will allow such a thing to happen to us, though. He is much too smart and cunning. Had King Jehoiakim listened to his counsel weeks ago, we would not be facing the sting of the Black Wind now. Instead, Jehoiakim declared his own siege on the royal family – making us prisoners in our own home. And now we are all under the siege of Nebuchadnezzar and his black army.

"I'm not afraid," I declared to Azariah earlier this afternoon. We had gone to the top of the city wall to observe the Babylonian army. "Jerusalem will not fall. The city is impenetrable. No one in history has breached its walls, and the Babylonians will not be the first," I declared.

Azariah didn't respond, he only stared at the sea of troops spread out in front of us. They carried on as far as the eye could see. Dotted pillars of campfire smoke numbered in the hundreds, maybe the thousands. Tents of various sizes have been erected, stables for horses have been constructed, a siege ramp is in its initial stages. The Babylonians are clearly here to stay.

In that moment, I doubted my own words. Yes, I am afraid. Very afraid. Azariah is too, as are all our friends and family. My mother cries every night. I can hear her sobs drifting from her bedchamber to mine. My sister is too young to understand, I think, but even she seems nervous.

How long this siege will last is anyone's guess, but I fear it will not end well.

A private entry in the Journal of Mishael
Twenty-first day of Tammuz, the third year of the reign of King Jehoiakim of Judah
The first year of the reign of King Nebuchadnezzar of Babylon
605 B.C.

-3-

It has not taken long for Nebuchadnezzar to sit on the throne in Jerusalem.

The Black Wind, indeed, is here to stay.

The siege ramp the Babylonians were building was unnecessary. King Jehoiakim, ever the politician whose concern is only himself and his own standing, sent a delegation to Nebuchadnezzar. An agreement was reached without an arrow being fired or fire being dropped. Judah is now a vassal state of the Babylonian Empire. True to his word, Jehoiakim has redirected the royal tribute once paid to Neco of Egypt and has now cast it into the Black Wind. In exchange, Jehoiakim remains in power, but as I wrote, it is Nebuchadnezzar who truly sits on the throne that oversees God's people.

I heard a man prophesying today outside the Temple. Someone I had not seen before.

"The judgement of God has arrived!" he cried. "The sins of the land have risen to the nostrils of God and he tolerates it no more. Jehoiakim has done evil in the sight of the Lord and now the Lord has delivered his answer. The Babylonians are the instrument of God's wrath against a people who have whored themselves with other gods!"

It was shocking to hear language like that being spoken on the Temple steps. Pashur, the priest, did not look happy. I asked Azariah who this man was, who dared to call out the sin of the people and the sin of King Jehoiakim in such public fashion.

"That is Jeremiah," he said. "King Jehoiakim hates that man."

So that was the great prophet Jeremiah, I thought. I had heard much about him, of his ravings and accusations against Jehoiakim and the Temple priests. "The man is mysterious and has few friends in the city," my own father had told me one night. Yet, he seems to draw a crowd when he prophesies, as was evidenced by the gathering today.

I found myself enthralled by his message. It was new and different. There was something about it that rang true to my ears. Jehoiakim is not a good king, that much is accepted by all. He remains in power because he allows everyone to do what is right in his own eyes. He challenges nothing with the Law of God. Surely Jeremiah is correct. God will not – cannot – tolerate the wickedness of his own people and the king forever.

So, now the Black Wind engulfs us. Jehoiakim has assured the city that nothing has changed. All will carry on as before - "Only now we will flourish under Nebuchadnezzar as opposed to Neco," he declared.

But it does not feel like we are flourishing. In fact, nothing about the Black Wind feels like rule under Neco of Egypt. As Azariah and I left the Temple area, we passed through the eastern market district of the city. Babylonian soldiers were having their way with the shop owners – taking food, leather goods, whatever they wanted, without paying.

I stared in horror from across the street of a bread shop owned by Benjamin, son of Obed. He is a gentle soul who bakes the most sumptuous challah and raisin-walnut babka. I've eaten from his counter my whole life. His daughter, Mary, is not much older than me, and I have always been partial to her. But being as I am a member of the royal family, it would not be proper for me to entertain thoughts of a courtship with her, although she is both sweet and beautiful.

A burly Babylonian man was pushing old Benjamin and throwing his breads into the street. The pushing intensified into a mild beating. The brute's friends stood and laughed as if it was nothing but sport. Benjamin's wife, Leah, came to his aid, also joined by Mary. Leah rushed to protect Benjamin from the blows of the soldier, while Mary – fearless Mary – walked up to the beast and slapped him across the face. He stopped his pounding on the old man and stared back at her. His eyes communicated, not anger at the slap, but hunger. And it was not a hunger for bread. The paw of his meaty hand took Mary by the mane of her hair and yanked her head back. She screamed as he ripped the top of her dress down, exposing her naked torso. He dragged Mary into the back of the shop. The only sound that followed were her screams for help. Benjamin and Leah cried out in agony as the group that had once served as spectators now held the couple back, helpless to do anything but listen and weep.

It appeared a line of soldiers was forming at the shop's entrance. My blood boiled. I wanted to do something, use my status as a royal to save Mary.

It would have been my death had I tried.

Sensing my foolishness, Azariah grabbed my arm and pulled me away. We ran back to the palace and to my house. I felt sick and my stomach relieved itself of its contents.

Azariah is worried about me. He has offered to stay the night with me and is sleeping across the room even now as I write this. He is a good friend.

A private entry in the Journal of Mishael
Tenth day of Av, the third year of the reign of King Jehoiakim of Judah
The first year of the reign of King Nebuchadnezzar of Babylon
605 B.C.

-4-

I spent today with Azariah and Hananiah. We gathered in the king's flower garden behind the garrison building. No one goes there, especially the Babylonians.

Father is busy in negotiations regarding the Babylonian occupation, and Mother is trying to distract my sister from our new reality.

All members of the royal family have been confined to the palace complex. "For your own safety," we are told by our new masters. But I've never felt unsafe walking the streets of Jerusalem...ever. Not until now, at least. Something is being planned. We all know it.

"There are fires burning throughout the city," Hananiah said. He sat on the ground wide-eyed as he shared the report. He'd snuck out of our shared "prison" the day before. He's only a year younger than me and Azariah, but he's small and skinny. He has a way of not being noticed.

"I can smell the smoke," I said. "I heard they are ordering the citizens to turn over any sort of weapons they might have and are burning them in the streets."

"That much is true, but they're burning homes and businesses too!"

"Please tell me that's not true, Hananiah." Azariah put his head in his hands.

"I wish it were not so, but it is. There's no rhyme or reason to the burning. I saw a group of soldiers gathered in the street. They were talking and numbering off the homes and shops. Then they spread out and began lighting fires. Totally random. They didn't give the owners any warning at all. They just lit torches and began throwing them on the roofs and inside the doorways. It was horrible. I saw one old woman throw a torch back at the solider who had tossed it into her home. He just laughed and then began to beat her until she didn't move anymore."

We sat in silence for a moment. I was tying the smell of the smoke in the air with the reality of what was actually happening to our beloved city. The City of God. But where was God in all of this? Had he abandoned us? Was that crazy old prophet, Jeremiah, right? Was this the judgement of God? But not all people in Jerusalem follow the ways of King Jehoiakim. Many of us still worship and offer sacrifices to Yahweh. My family keeps Passover every year. We pray the Shema every morning and every night. We keep the Sabbath. My father says that God's protective hand may have left Judah, but Yahweh still watches over His people, always looking for those who are faithful to Him. He sees and knows and He will protect His own. "Like a shepherd taking care of his sheep," he says.

But I don't know if I agree with that anymore. It doesn't feel like God is watching over any of us anymore.

"There are stories that the women of the city are being raped by the Babylonians as well, and I think that's true," Hananiah said, breaking the silence.

I thought of Mary and felt ashamed. I think Azariah sensed my unspoken shame because he gave my shoulder a squeeze.

"And the Temple treasure is being looted."

"What?!" Azariah shouted a little too loudly. "That's a sacrilege. Surely, they know that."

"That's exactly why they're doing it," I said, finally finding my tongue. "They are hitting us in every place that hurts. Burning the shops and the homes of the people. Not all of them, just enough to send a message. Taking our women for themselves. The Temple treasure is just another symbol of their power. Mighty Babylon is greater than Yahweh."

"You shouldn't say such things, Mishael."

"I'm not saying I believe it, or that it's even true. I'm just saying that's the message the Black Wind carries with it." I understood Hananiah's scolding of me. It could seem blasphemous to utter such things, even if one was only relaying the sentiment of another.

"I've also heard talk of an exile," I said.

The mouth of Azariah gaped open, about to respond, but Hananiah beat him to it. "Surely not! King Jehoiakim has come to an agreement with them. He's agreed to pay the tribute and has pledged himself to Nebuchadnezzar. There's no need for an exile."

"I heard them talking about it," I continued. "My father, King Jehoiakim, and there was a Babylonian eunuch present. His name is Ashpenaz and he apparently is very close to Nebuchadnezzar and has been granted authority by him. It's all about securing power. Making sure that we won't rebel once the army returns to Babylon."

"An exile," Azariah repeated. "I wonder who they will select."

I didn't say anything more in the moment. But I already knew. I'd overheard them talking about that as well.

"Has anyone spoken with Daniel?" Hananiah asked. "We should find Daniel and see what he thinks about all of this."

It was a good idea. Daniel is only a couple of years older than us, but he is wise beyond his years. I think tomorrow I will try to find Daniel.

A private entry in the Journal of Mishael
Fifteenth day of Av, the third year of the reign of King Jehoiakim of Judah
The first year of the reign of King Nebuchadnezzar of Babylon
605 B.C.

-5-

I found Daniel early this morning on the royal porch just outside the court of the Gentiles. I could not sleep at all last night so I rose early to take a walk, intending to offer a sacrifice at the Temple. I had thought to purchase a turtle dove as an offering to Yahweh, but knowing it was too early for the markets of the royal porch to be open, I had decided to simply walk, and pray, and wait. That's when I saw Daniel. He seemed to be walking and praying and waiting as well.

When he saw me approaching, his face brightened. "Good morning, Mishael. Yahweh Shalom."

The Lord is peace. I shook my head. "Good morning to you as well, Daniel. If only it were still true." I said in response to his greeting.

Daniel furrowed his brow. "What troubles you, my

friend? You look like you're carrying the weight of a millstone around your neck."

My lack of sleep must have been showing. And perhaps more. "The same thing that troubles us all. The Babylonians. Perhaps the Lord is peace, but if so, then He has departed Jerusalem, for there is no peace any longer in this city."

"And yet I sense you are here this morning to obtain a sacrifice to offer Him in His Holy Temple. Am I right?" He nodded toward Solomon's Temple where the priests were now awake and beginning preparations for the day. "I'm not so sure you actually believe your own words."

"I don't know what to believe anymore." I looked down, ashamed of my doubt.

"Yahweh does not change, Mishael. He is the same yesterday, today, and forever."

"You sound like a prophet, Daniel."

He laughed out loud at the suggestion. "I'm only two years older than you. And my family are of the royal class, the same as yours. The prophets come from the countryside. You know that."

He was dodging me with his words. "Have you had any new dreams lately?"

Everyone knew that Daniel had dreams. Strange dreams that seemed to have no meaning at all. He'd stopped talking about them some time ago because most of our peers just made fun of them. Even his parents did not think them to be of consequence. But a few of us believed there was more to the dreams – *visions* as Daniel, at times, referred to them. Daniel was the same as the rest of us, but he was also different. He was more introspective than most people whose years were numbered in the teens. It didn't bother him to be alone. In fact, he seemed to prefer it. Yet, one never felt he was bothering Daniel if he approached him. Because of this, Daniel was always the go-to for advice among his peers. I'd even heard rumors that some older men sought his counsel, or at least his perspective.

At the mention of dreams, Daniel became forlorn in his appearance. His shoulders sagged a bit and we walked in silence.

"Now you look like the one who has a millstone tied around his neck," I finally said.

"If you must know, yes, I have had a dream. The same dream, in fact, for several nights now. I wake up and cannot get the images out of my head. So, rather than lay in bed, I get up and a take a walk. Many times, walking can help me sort out the meaning."

"That is why you are here so early this morning, isn't it? You had this dream again last night and so you've come for a walk."

He laughed again, his mood lightening. "Now you sound like a prophet, Mishael."

"But you did have the dream last night, didn't you?"

"Yes, I did," he admitted.

"Tell me about it. What do you think it means?"

"What it means I am still trying to sort out. But the dream itself: It is the season of harvest. The wheat crop is full and ready, but a great fire is sweeping the land from the East. There is a cry from the people to save the crops and so everyone joins in the harvest. The people toil day and night. Men, women, children. Widows and orphans. Young and old. Rich and poor. All people of all classes take part in the great harvest, for everyone knows that if the wheat is burned then no one will eat. And it is a success. The wheat is brought in and the people are secure. Yet the fire still comes. So, the master of the harvest, the one who planted the seed, he orders that stalks of harvested wheat be selected. And not just any stalks. He orders the best of the best be collected and the set out in front of the fire to be consumed. The fire comes and rages and consumes the stalks of wheat set out as a sacrifice. And once the wheat is consumed, the fire ceases."

We had stopped walking as he narrated the tale of his vision. I was transfixed by the imagery. I knew with certainty this was no ordinary dream. It meant something. Something important. And it felt close to home, personal even.

"What do you think it means, Daniel? What is the interpretation of the dream?"

"I don't know, Mishael. What do you think it means?"

"You want me to play the prophet, Daniel? You want me to be the interpreter of dreams?"

"I'm just asking you what you think it means, is all." He eyed me with a knowing stare.

"I've heard talk of an exile," I made myself say.

"As have I."

"The Babylonians have gathered all of us of the noble class into the royal district. We are limited in where we can go in the city now."

"Yes we are."

"And I don't think they are done."

"Neither do I."

An overwhelming sense of exhaustion overcame me.

Maybe it was the lack of sleep catching up to me. Maybe it was what I knew was coming next. "You and I are the stalks of fine wheat, aren't we?" Daniel only offered a gentle smile. "The exile is happening soon and you and I – and some others as well – will soon be headed to Babylon." There it was. I had finally said it. Out loud. An act of admission.

Daniel put his arm around my shoulder. "Come on, Mishael. Let's go offer our sacrifices to Yahweh."

A private entry in the Journal of Mishael
Sixteenth day of Av, the third year of the reign of King Jehoiakim of Judah
The first year of the reign of King Nebuchadnezzar of Babylon
605 B.C.

-6-

Today the waiting finally ended.

A Babylonian eunuch accompanied by two guards arrived on the doorstep of our home at dawn. He'd been sent by Ashpenaz, chief of the eunuchs, with the following order:

All young men of nobility, ages thirteen to eighteen, are required to gather two hours before the sun is at its highest in the courtyard of the royal palace. Bring nothing with you except one bag. By order of the Great King – King Nebuchadnezzar of the Babylonian Empire as executed by Ashpenaz of the eunuchs.

My mother broke down into sobs. My father asked to see the order himself – as if seeing the words in ink on parchment would change the contents of the order. I merely returned to my room to pack my bag: a few clothes, a copy of the Law of God, a dagger my father gave me when I turned fourteen, and, of course, my journal. And then I sat and waited.

At the appointed hour, I left my room to find my parents and sister gathered in the main room of our home. They'd chosen to leave me to myself and my preparations, but with my emergence my mother's tears began to roll down her cheeks again. I was determined to remain strong.

My father embraced me and then, pulling away, he placed his large hand on the side of my face. A look of sadness like I'd never seen before shown in his dark brown eyes. I will never forget that look.

My mother came to me next. She carried a linen cloth wrapped around a small object. She pressed it into my hand and enveloped me into a smothering hug. She whispered in my ear, "This is a Mezuzah. I have saved it for the day you married and had your own home. But you must take it now," her voice broke, "to your new home. Remember the words of the Shema that are written on the parchment inside it. No matter where the road leads, always, always remember: The Lord our God is one God. Love the Lord, Mishael. Love Him with your whole heart, and soul, and strength. Never forget these words."

And with that she pulled back. My sister, Ruth, gave me a hug as well. She is clearly too young to understand what is happening. I kept myself from saying goodbye to her – a feeble attempt on my part – allowing her to remain as long as possible in her world of innocence.

Father put his arm around me and together we left for the courtyard.

There were no less than one hundred of us gathered. We were summarily placed in lines of twenty-five, four rows deep. I was on the third row.

My father, along with the other fathers, stood clumped to the side. A regiment of Babylonian soldiers formed a ring around the courtyard.

No one spoke.

A lone man in a flowing black robe and an ornate headwrap walked toward the first row of us.

It was Ashpenaz.

I had heard him speak of this day to King Jehoiakim while hiding in the recesses of the royal court. I had read his order earlier in the morning, commanding the presence of all the young men of Judah's nobility. And now he was this close. Only feet from me. The Black Wind incarnate.

"Today is a day of selection," he shouted. His voice echoed around the boundaries where we were gathered. "I have been ordered by the Great King Nebuchadnezzar to select the best of you. The Great King demands nothing but the finest of every land he conquers!"

The boy standing next to me let out a whimper. I felt sorry for him as he appeared to have only recently come of age. I didn't even know his name.

"Only the most fortunate among you will be chosen to go with me to Babylon. You will be given the finest education in the empire. The finest food. The finest of the arts. The finest that the Great King has to offer. You will want for nothing. The rest of you, those found unworthy of the Great King's benevolence, will remain in this most cursed of lands. You will be allowed to carry on with your pitiful existence. And let today be a message to all the people of this horrid place: The Great King takes what he wants. All the world is his and there is nothing in it that does not belong to him. Today we take only your young men. Should you rebel, we will return and take the rest!"

Ashpenaz's speech ended with a thunderous shout and stomp from the Babylonian army surrounding the whole scene. It was enough to make us all flinch.

The selection process began. A glimmer of hope had risen inside of me as Ashpenaz had rattled on. Perhaps I would be blessed by Yahweh and be passed over – allowed to return to my family.

Ashpenaz did not take long in making his choices. He moved quickly down each row with a guard behind him. He would pass three or four boys and then he would pause in front of another. A jerk of his head was the indication that a selection had been made and the guard would yank the chosen one out of line and push him across the courtyard toward the far side.

No one resisted.

The fourth selection caught my attention. It was Azariah. He hung his head as he made the long walk to join the other three. On the second row, Hananiah was chosen. He had always been good at not being seen, but that skill failed him today. And then came the third row. Ashpenaz walked more quickly this time, as if he was tired of the whole process. He simply pointed arbitrarily at individuals as he moved. They were summarily yanked out of line.

My heart beat fast as he moved closer to me. I prayed he would walk on past, but my prayers failed to reach Yahweh.

He stopped in front of me and looked me fully up and down. He was a towering figure. His beady eyes were black as the wind that carried him to the Holy City. His moist lips, ringed by a dark goatee, curled into a wicked smile.

A jerk of his head and I found myself being jerked out of line.

I made the long walk to join the others as Ashpenaz was finishing the final row. He'd stopped and was spending an unusually long amount of time standing in front of a young man we could not see. It appeared a conversation was taking place. Next came the signature jerk of his head and then Ashpenaz walked away from the group. The selection process was finished. It appeared there were thirty of us in all. The last one chosen was still walking toward us...Daniel.

"We leave immediately!" Ashpenaz finished the way he started - with a shout.

And so we did. We were summarily escorted to a waiting caravan and marched out of the city. The last thing I saw as we left the courtyard was the face of my father. He looked as if life itself had been stripped from him.

A great multitude of the Babylonian army are leaving with us, returning to the capital of the empire. It will take many months to make the journey, we have been told.

Today is the worst day of my life. I can't imagine there could be any worse in the days ahead. My only console is that my two best friends are with me. I feel sorry for Azariah and Hananiah, but at least we are together.

And thank Yahweh that Daniel is with us too.

We will see what tomorrow brings.

A private entry in the Journal of Mishael
Twenty-first day of Av, the third year of the reign of King Jehoiakim of Judah
The first year of the reign of King Nebuchadnezzar of Babylon
605 B.C.

-7-

We have been traveling across the wilderness for four days.

It is hot, miserable, and I miss my family and home. I am trying to be brave, especially for Hananiah. He's not doing well at all. Azariah is trying to be brave as well but I can see the sadness on his face.

We are all sad.

Our captors are not cruel, but neither are they gracious. For all the talk of Ashpenaz at the selection days ago — about how we would lack for nothing — what we lack is the compassion of the Black Wind. But what were we to expect? We are the inferior race. The look of disdain from each and every solider and eunuch is obvious. Ashpenaz is the worst of all. One of the younger ones named Aaron was weeping as we traveled today. Ashpenaz walked to him and slapped the boy hard.

"You ungrateful little worm. Never weep in my sight!" He finished the rebuke by spitting in his face.

I believe he would whip us all for the mere pleasure of it, were it not for King Nebuchadnezzar's command that we be taken good care of on our passage to Babylon. I am convinced they have some plan for us when we arrive. I just do not know what it is.

Each night, after we finally stop for the day, have eaten, and bedded down...I cry. I can hear the sounds of the other boys crying as well. Just a few minutes ago, I dared to sit up, deciding to try to write something down about these first few days.

I caught sight of Daniel just a few sleeping bodies over from me. He's sitting up too, but he's not crying. He's praying. I think I will pray as well after I close this journal.

A private entry in the Journal of Mishael
Twenty-sixth day of Av, the third year of the reign of King Jehoiakim of Judah
The first year of the reign of King Nebuchadnezzar of Babylon
605 B.C.

-8-

We arrive in Babylon only two days from now.

It has been a long journey. Longer than I could ever have imagined. We have been traveling for one hundred and thirty-eight days. It has been a hard drive – the goal, we were told, was to complete the journey before winter. We have succeeded.

I have had no desire to write of the miseries of this trek. It has been one long day after another without variation.

I have lost some weight, which is to be expected I suppose. And I am in the best physical shape of my life. Walking ten to fifteen miles a day works to sculpt the body, it seems. And true to their word, our captors have made sure we've been well fed. In fact, we eat better than the soldiers who have guided our way. I am certain that only adds to the disdain they feel toward us, but I don't care. I didn't ask for any of this. I can't help but think my family would be pleased if they could see me. Oh, how I miss them.

I've found a rhythm to my days. I talk to my friends, mostly Azariah and Hananiah. And I talk to Yahweh. In fact, I have found an unexpected sweetness in communing with my God for hours on end as I tread across His creation. I had always thought that Yahweh could only be accessed directly through the sacrificial system of the Temple in Jerusalem. But I have come to see that God is much bigger than the Temple. The whole world truly is his footstool and His reach has no limits. But what about Babylon? Will I be able to hear him from that wicked city?

I must admit – there is a slight thrill rising in my spirit at the anticipation of seeing Babylon. That thrill is tinged with fear as well. None of us knows anything about what lies before us in that great city, but we are tired of this campaign across the world and ready to see what this new home will have to offer us.

A private entry in the Journal of Mishael
Eleventh day of Tishrei, the third year of the reign of King Jehoiakim of Judah

The first year of the reign of King Nebuchadnezzar of Babylon
605 B.C.

-9-

"You are now citizens of Babylon!"

Ashpenaz seemed in a profoundly better mood this morning, the day after our arrival in the city. And oh, what a city it is. I could never have imagined a place so beautiful and so ugly at the same time. The architecture of the buildings, the clothes people wear, the smells of the foods cooking in the air, the music drifting from the entertainment district – it is all intoxicating. But the shrines to gods I have never heard of are everywhere. Every street corner, every rooftop, it seems, has a dedicated altar of worship on it. I thought Jerusalem had embraced paganism under Jehoiakim – and it had – but Jerusalem is nothing like this place.

"The fruits of the Land of Shinar are yours!" Ashpenaz continued his speech.

The thirty of us taken captive were gathered in a

common area outside the small building where we'd been assigned rooms. Each living quarter houses four to five people and we were allowed to group up as we wished. Azariah and Hananiah quickly grouped with me. When all was done, only one of us was left alone: Daniel. The oldest and wisest of us all. He seemed in no rush, perfectly content come what may. Our eyes met and he smiled, joining us as if he'd expected it to be this way all along.

Our accommodations are exceedingly nice. And new robes in the style of the Chaldeans were waiting on us. It feels so strange to wear them, but my Jewish robes will no longer do. They are in tatters after the nearly four-month journey.

"The Great King Nebuchadnezzar has ordered that the finest foods from his table be given to you. Meats of every variety, breads, fruits, vegetables, and the king's private stock of the finest wine. You are indeed a blessed group of young men. Additionally, you will be enrolled immediately into the royal academy of Babylon. The best tutors will instruct you in the wonders of the world. You will learn mathematics and the sciences. You will become proficient in our language, the language of the gods. And you will be immersed in the glory of Babylonian art and literature. Some of you will undoubtedly become artisans and poets yourselves. Some will become scientists and architects."

This is the strangest captivity. Unlike what I had anticipated. Fresh baths, fine clothes, even servants in our quarters. No want for food, and an education never thought of back in Jerusalem. And most surprising of all – no chains. Not one time, from the moment we left the selection back in Jerusalem, were the shackles of iron applied.

"The Great King requires only two things in exchange for these great gifts. You must first and foremost bow to the King. Worship whatever god you choose, but the Great Nebuchadnezzar is the one you bow before. And secondly, give back to Babylon. The expectation is that you will contribute to the betterment of our city and the empire."

Ashpenaz smiled and I thought his speech was concluded. I was wrong. "Now," he began again, "it is time for the renaming."

Renaming? I looked at Azariah and Hananiah and they seemed as confused as me. Daniel's face was unreadable.

"You have left behind the filth of your Hebrew upbringing. What was, is no more. You have been reborn. And as such, you will each be given a new name. A Babylonian name. This new name will become your identity.

It will *be* the new you."

And with that, Ashpenaz retreated to a small tent and took a seat on a large cushioned chair. One by one we each went before him and a new name was given.

After dinner, the four of us gathered in our quarters. It was the first moment we had been able to be back together after a full day of touring the city and meeting our tutors.

"Azariah, what is your *new* name?!" Hananiah was picking on Azariah, making fun of the whole process from earlier in the day. Azariah didn't take it very well. "Come on, spit it out. What is it?"

"Abednego," he replied somberly.

"Abednego," Hananiah repeated. "I guess that's not so bad. It has a nice ring to it. It's better than mine for sure. Shadrach! Can you believe that? What kind of name is Shadrach? Ashpenaz told me my name means *command of Aku, the moon god*. That's stupid as far as I'm concerned. I am no servant of the moon god, I can tell you that."

Hananiah - or Shadrach it was now, I suppose - was being awfully chatty. He continued, "What does Abednego mean, Azariah? It has to be better than moon god."

"He told me it means *servant of Nebo*." Azariah's face turned red. "I am no servant of Nebo. My name is Azariah.

The name my parents gave me. Ashpenaz asked me what my name means, and when I told him Azariah means *Yahweh will help*, he gave me that horrible smile of his and said, 'Your God has obviously failed you. No need to keep the name Azariah any longer.' That's when he told me I would now be known as the servant of Nebo. Abednego." Azariah spat on the floor.

"What about you, Daniel? What's your new name?" Hananiah shifted his attention from Azariah. I think he was trying to break the tension of the moment.

"I am now Beltshazzar. A name that appeals to the Babylonian god Marduk for the protection of my life."

He said it so easily, as if it didn't bother him at all. But he wasn't making light of it in the way that Hananiah had.

"And what about you, Mishael. What is your name now?"

"He sat me down as well," I began. "Ashpenaz asked me the same question as Azariah. He wanted to know my name and what it meant. I told him that Mishael means that there is none like Yahweh. And yes, I got the wicked smile as well. He mocked Yahweh and then gave me my new name. A name that means: *There is none like Aku*. The moon god." I looked at Hananiah. "My name is Meshach."

A private entry in the Journal of Mishael

Fifteenth day of Tishrei, the third year of the reign of King Jehoiakim of Judah

The first year of the reign of King Nebuchadnezzar of Babylon

605 B.C.

-10-

"We cannot eat the king's food."

It was the most animated I have ever seen Daniel. We were all gathered at our breakfast table this morning. The first full day with our new names. In front of us was an array of pork, beef, cheese, fruits, nuts, and grains. It looked delicious but I was acutely aware of the kosher laws of the Torah. It seemed clear, however, that there was an expectation from those serving us: We were to eat.

"They can change our names. They can change our dress. They can teach us their language and teach us all manner of academic disciplines. None of that concerns me. All truth flows from Yahweh no matter the source. And clothes and names are but window dressing. Yes, they are trying to remold us, to shape us into something new and away from that which we are. But they cannot change our hearts.

Take the new name or don't take it, it matters little to me and, I think, to God. But our bodies must remain strong and fit. For an unfit body will lead to an unfit mind. And an unfit mind will threaten to compromise the heart."

Where this version of Daniel had come from, I did not know. He has always been the wisest of us, which is why we all listened when he speaks. It's just that he doesn't speak often, and never in monologue fashion. We continued with rapt attention.

"This," he pointed to the buffet in front of us, "this is the recipe of indulgence and sloth. To eat this combination of food, three times a day, day after day, will break our wills. It will change us. So, I have made my decision and I invite you, my brothers, to join me. Let it be a pact among just us. We will only eat fruits and vegetables. And we will partake of no wine."

The Babylonian steward in charge of the meals heard Daniel speaking and confronted him, with everyone listening.

"Why are you so ungrateful for the King's hospitality? He expects, no he demands, that the lot of you just arrived from Jerusalem be given the best of his stores. That you grow strong and exhibit vitality. How would this be possible if you withhold the meat and the wine? And then I will be held accountable to Ashpenaz and ultimately King Nebuchadnezzar himself. I appeal to you. Eat!"

The steward's name is Koran and he seems to be a kind soul. His appeal was as much for his own safety as it was ours, I think.

"Let us come to an agreement." I was amazed at how Daniel took charge of the situation. "Give us nothing but fruits and vegetables and water for ten days. Then compare us with the others. If we have declined, then we will relent and all will be well. But if we compare as equals, then what is the harm?"

It seemed reasonable to Koran and he took the meat and wine from us. A compromise had been reached. Daniel smiled at the three of us. "Well, what are you waiting for? Let's eat!"

A private entry in the Journal of Mishael
Sixteenth day of Tishrei, the third year of the reign of King Jehoiakim of Judah
The first year of the reign of King Nebuchadnezzar of Babylon
605 B.C.

-11-

I never would have thought I would be a vegetarian!

"Anything that grows from a seed," declared Daniel.

The last ten days have not been as hard as I thought they would be. Our diet of vegetables, fruit, grains, and various breads has provided surprising sustenance. Oh, I miss the chicken and beef and lamb I'd come to enjoy back home, but I can feel myself growing stronger and feeling well. My complexion has even cleared.

The others agree with me. Azariah – or I suppose I should say, Abednego (we are still getting used to our new names) – was the most vocal about not going along, but he relented to some friendly pressure applied by myself and Shadrach.

And who could say no to Daniel?

He has become our leader of sorts. I have a hard time

thinking of him as Belteshazzar. I think he will always just be Daniel to me.

This morning after breakfast our steward, Koran, called us to the courtyard before our studies were to begin. He lined us up and looked us over. He powered both of his hands in a strong slap on my shoulders. He took his time, having me hold my arms out, examining the tone of my muscles, looking over my legs, and even looking in my mouth with my tongue wagging out.

Such was the same with all of us.

"I would not have thought it possible," he began by way of summary after the examination, "but you four look as fit as any and better than most. Are you certain you've not secretly indulged yourself with meat and wine?"

"You set our table each meal, good Koran." Daniel took the lead by way of an answer. "And you remove what is left after we are done. Nothing happens outside your watchful eye. It is as I said. Let us have ten days eating the food we choose – only that which grows from the ground – and you judge for yourself if we are not healthy and well."

"Oh, you are healthy and well, that is not up for dispute. I must admit, I am surprised. But Ashpenaz will be pleased as will the Great King Nebuchadnezzar."

"So, we have your permission to continue?"

"You do," Koran nodded. "Now hurry to your studies."

Our spirits were on a new high the rest of the day. As I write this, I think I will admit that I feel better physically than I have in my entire life.

Daniel seems pleased as well. He says that Yahweh has chosen us. That God is preparing us for something important.

I can't imagine what. But so far, Daniel has been correct about everything.

A private entry in the Journal of Mishael
Twenty-sixth day of Tishrei, the third year of the reign of King Jehoiakim of Judah
The first year of the reign of King Nebuchadnezzar of Babylon
605 B.C.

-12-

Tomorrow we stand before King Nebuchadnezzar.

I am so nervous but not sure as to why. Surely the king has nothing but good will prepared for us. Ashpenaz says we have all done well - all thirty of us taken from our homes in Jerusalem.

It has only been three years but it seems a lifetime ago. I have trouble remembering the faces of my mother and father and sister at times. But then Yahweh will grant me a dream and there they are, smiling at me, and I remember them once again.

Our studies in the academy are done. Ashpenaz has declared there is no more that we can learn. The Akkadian language has become second nature to us. I will admit, I have obtained the best education in the empire, better than had I stayed in Judah. It was obvious from the beginning that the goal of the Great King was to strip us of our former selves – our identities, our personalities, our families, our God. But I can testify that for me and my friends, he has not succeeded.

Maybe that is why I am nervous to stand before him tomorrow. Maybe he will see that his great effort has been for naught. Everyone knows not to anger Nebuchadnezzar. His temper is legendary and he disposes of those who challenge him like most men would swat a gnat – with great ease and without a second thought.

While I am still the same man I was three years ago – yes I am now a man, having reached the age of eighteen – two things have changed by my way of thinking.

First, the three of us have embraced the names: Shadrach, Meshach, and Abednego.

It started off as a game among us. Calling each other by our assigned Babylonian names while we were in private, just as a way to make fun and to poke at one another. But over time, they began to stick. I am still Mishael, but I am also Meshach. I guess I view it as a nickname of sorts.

But Daniel remains Daniel to us all. The Babylonians still call him Belteshazzar, but nothing about that name sounds right to us.

And second, I've embraced the Babylonian calendar and their way of reckoning time in all my journal entries. Since I will never again live in Judah, it makes no sense to hold on to a way of reckoning time that does not fit the world in which I now live.

I struggled with this at first and went to Daniel for his advice. A lot of people, both Jew and Babylonian, go to Daniel for advice it seems.

"A calendar is but a man-made instrument," he told me. "As are the names we call one another. Don't be overly concerned with such things, Meshach." He gave me a wink as he called me by my Babylonian name. "It's important to know what day it is, and it's important to know who you are. But it's infinitely more important to know who your God is."

That seems like good advice given who we will stand before tomorrow.

A private entry in the Journal of Meshach
Fourth day of Kislimu, the second year of the reign of King
Nebuchadnezzar of Babylon
602 B.C.

-13-

"Ashpenaz! What brings you before me today and what rabble is this you drag in here with you?" King Nebuchadnezzar bellowed. His voice echoed around the chamber of the awesome throne room. I have not seen wealth like the wealth surrounding this king.

Nebuchadnezzar seemed in a foul mood when we first arrived before his court. Perched on his gold-laden throne, he was dealing with a matter of dishonesty among his private house staff. Apparently, a steward was accused of stealing, and additional rumors swirled that he had acted inappropriately toward one of the king's daughters.

The king asked no questions of the steward after the charges were read. His face grew red and he summarily ordered the man's execution. To be carried out immediately. The man screamed and begged for his life as he was led from the room. The sound of a sword could be heard being drawn from its sheath and then the screaming ceased.

Nebuchadnezzar seemed to not notice at all and called for the next item of business. Over the course of the hour, various matters were brought before the king. There was an issue with taxes. A report was brought from one of the generals regarding the occupation of Judah. This caused the thirty of us – me and my fellow Jews exiled three years prior – to perk up. We stood at the back of the throne room, waiting our turn. According to the general, Jehoiakim was behaving himself, although his attitude toward the Babylonian occupation had soured some.

And then it came time for Ashpenaz to come forward with the lot of us in tow.

"Oh, Great King!" he began. "Before you come the exiles of Judah. Thirty men of *former* nobility. Because of your gracious kindness, they have received the finest education in all the world. They have dined from your table for these past three years and they are now prepared to enter your service as the king deems."

"Three years, you say? My how time has grown wings and flown from us all!" He gave a hearty laugh. Ashpenaz smiled, seemingly pleased with the king's demeanor.

Whatever I had expected standing before King Nebuchadnezzar for the first time, this was not it. It seemed his attitude could flip from anger, to joy, to apathy, to irritation, and there was no way to predict from one moment to the next which Nebuchadnezzar one would get.

Thinking of the poor soul who had been so easily dispatched with, I too, was glad he was laughing.

"Bring them forward, then," the king commanded, waving his arm in a motion that said come. "Let me see them for myself and judge what caliber of job you've done with this rabble from the Judean wilderness, my good Ashpenaz." He laughed again.

We came forward. All thirty of us in three lines of ten.

The king came off his perch and approached us directly. He walked back and forth, up and down each row. He nodded, gave a grunt occasionally, asked a few questions of Ashpenaz regarding the training we'd been given, and even quizzed a few of us. I was so nervous, I stood like a statue, not moving a muscle in my body.

After a period of time - I have no idea how long - he moved to stand in front of the whole group of us.

His eyes fell on me. On me! He stared at me long and hard.

I could tell he was thinking. But of what, I had no idea. He finally shifted his gaze to another. Time stood still once again. He did this yet again. And then a fourth time.

"Ashpenaz!"

"Yes, my good king!" Ashpenaz had turned pale in the face. Something was wrong and the chief of the eunuchs sensed it as well.

"I believe we have a problem."

"A problem, my king?"

"These four! You." He pointed at me. My heart sank. "And you." His finger pointed at another. "And this one also and then you." He singled out two others. Four in all. "Come forward. The four of you. Stand in front of me."

I closed my eyes and took a nervous step out of line. What had I done? Why had I stuck out? I made my way forward, as did three others. I dared not look to either side for fear of disrespecting the Great King who held my life in his hands. I came to stand in front of Nebuchadnezzar, as did three others to my left.

"And who, pray tell, are these four, Ashpenaz? Tell me quickly!"

"Their names are: Shadrach, Meshach, Abednego, and Belteshazzar."

What? How was that possible? I dared a glance to my left and it was true. My two best friends and Daniel stood in line with me. Come what may, I felt brave in that moment.

"These four..." he paused as if trying to find the words. "These four are different. They look healthier than the others. There is something about them I can't quite discern. But I like them!" He laughed big and loud. I felt myself carried along in the surreal nature of the moment. "How have they done in their studies, Ashpenaz?"

"They are the finest of the lot, my king. There are none better."

"Yes. I can see it." He eyed us each individually once again. "I want them close to me, Ashpenaz. These four. Have them transferred immediately to the company of my magicians and enchanters. I have grown weary of the counsel that group gives me at times. We need new blood among them." He paused one last time and then said, "And these four *former* nobles may be just what I need in the days to come."

The king was done and swept with haste out of the room.

I turned to look at my friends. They were as stunned as I was.

And then I looked at Daniel. He only smiled and gave me a wink.

A private entry in the Journal of Meshach
Fifth day of Kislimu, the second year of the reign of King
Nebuchadnezzar of Babylon
602 B.C.

-14-

Shadrach, Abednego and I went to the Plain of Dura today to see for ourselves the building of the massive statue that King Nebuchadnezzar has ordered. It will be in the image of...of course, Nebuchadnezzar.

The work has only begun and it is clear it will be a monstrosity. The craftsmen are busy at work fashioning various body parts of wood all across the worksite of the plain. It is a strange site. An arm here, a leg there. All massive in size. The feet are complete and have been overlaid with gold. I stood next to one and it was taller than me. Just a foot! When the whole thing is finished and covered in gold, it will surely be a wonder of the world.

"Would you look at it, my brothers?" Shadrach asked. "Only a king with the ego of Nebuchadnezzar would order the building of such a thing."

"Yes, only Nebuchadnezzar," agreed Abednego. "I think he thinks he is a god." He finished by throwing a stone at the golden foot.

I cautioned him, looking around to see if anyone had observed the sign of disrespect. "You must be careful, Abednego!" I chided. "The king has eyes everywhere. His mood is hard to predict, swinging from joyous to furious in the same hour. I think him to be one easily thrown to fits of rage."

My words would ring true much sooner than I could have imagined. When we arrived back to the royal grounds where we now live, Daniel was looking for us. There was a frantic nature to him which immediately captured our attention. Daniel is never frantic.

"I have just spoken with Arioch, the king's captain," Daniel began. "A decree has been issued from Nebuchadnezzar. A decree of death." His eyes were wide with what looked like fear. "The king has ordered all of his wise men and counselors put to death. He is in a rage."

My mind clouded over in that moment. "All of the king's wise men? His whole counsel?" I asked. "Well that includes us, Daniel. *We* are a part of the king's counsel."

"This can't be right!" Shadrach erupted. "It makes no sense. Why would he issue such an order?"

"The king is undone, I say," Daniel continued. "Captain Arioch says that the king has had a dream. A dream that has torn him asunder. He is all out of sorts and he demands that his wise men tell him what the dream is and provide an interpretation."

"Tell him what the dream is?" I asked. "Can't *he* at least do that much? Surely if he provides the details of his dream, someone can offer a reasonable explanation for its meaning."

"And that is the problem, Meshach. The king *can't remember* the dream."

We looked at Daniel, confused.

"Haven't you ever had a dream, brothers? A dream that took hold of you and seemed oh, so real? But the moment you woke, the images and details slipped from your mind like sand through your fingers?"

I nodded, understanding coming to me at Daniel's explanation.

"Well, that is what has happened to Nebuchadnezzar. He has had a dream. A powerful dream that has shaken him. He is convinced it means something and he is desperate to know what. But he cannot even remember what the dream was. And since no one in his counsel can tell him the dream and its meaning, he has ordered us all killed."

"What are we going to do?" I asked.

"We are going to pray, my brothers. I've sent a message to King Nebuchadnezzar through Captain Arioch. I've told the king that I will tell him the content of his dream and its meaning."

"You *what*?!" We all shouted at once.

"Such a thing is not possible," Abednego moaned.

"We are doomed. We are all doomed." Shadrach began to weep.

"We are not doomed," I said, more boldly than I felt. The others looked at me. "At least not yet. Daniel has bought us time. He is right." I looked at Daniel and gave him a nod. "We will pray. We will call out to Yahweh for mercy. All things are possible with God. Even the dreams of a king are not hidden from him. So, we will pray. And then Daniel will sleep. And perhaps he will dream too."

A private entry in the Journal of Meshach
Tenth day of Šabatu, the third year of the reign of King
Nebuchadnezzar of Babylon
601 B.C.

-15-

The rooster crowed and Daniel's eyes shot open. He bolted from his bed and ran from the house we all shared. His only cry was, "I must see the king!" And then he was gone.

Sometime in the early hours of morning I must have drifted off while praying, for my eyes opened as well to the sunrise call of the rooster. I had no time to confer with Daniel before he was gone.

Shadrach and Abednego were both snoring until I kicked them. "Wake up, the two of you! Daniel has had a vision from God and has gone to see the king." I was only guessing, of course, but what else could it be? One thing was for certain, had Daniel not seen a vision and been given the contents of the dream of Nebuchadnezzar and its meaning, then today would be our last day on earth. Our death had been decreed.

So, we prayed. Oh, how we prayed. Like I never have before in my entire life. Even the night before the Babylonians came for us back in Jerusalem, I did not pray this hard. We cried out to Yahweh to save us, certainly, but there was something else that transpired among the three of us as we sat huddled together, our arms around one another in prayer.

Peace.

Calm.

Serenity.

I know it sounds strange, but in these months that we have been in exile in Babylon, I actually feel closer to God rather than further from him. I had always been taught that Yahweh dwells in Jerusalem – in the Temple itself inside the Holy of Holies on top of the Bema Seat. Yet, I can sense Yahweh's presence here in Babylon as surely as I could in Jerusalem – even more so, if I am honest. And this is without me offering any sort of sacrifices at the Temple at all.

The prophet Isaiah once claimed that God asked the question of our people: "What makes you think I want all your sacrifices?" And then Isaiah claimed that God declared by way of an answer: "I am sick of your burnt offerings of rams and the fat of your fattened cattle. I get no pleasure from the blood of bulls and lambs and goats."

It seemed like near blasphemy at the time, that Isaiah would put such words in the mouth of Yahweh. But perhaps God really was speaking to him. I will likely never offer a sacrifice again to God in the Temple. How can I? Yet, God seems more real to me now than ever before.

If it was for me to die today, I think I would have embraced it, for it would only have meant I would be with my God.

But such was not the case! Daniel returned in early afternoon with great fanfare. Captain Arioch was with him as were a handful of guards.

"Pack your belongings, my friends!" he commanded. "We are all leaving."

Panic struck for but a moment. I thought that we were being led to the execution. But then, why pack our things?

Seeing the confusion on our collective faces, Daniel explained, "Yahweh has answered our prayers... and more!" His smile was infectious. "I dreamed, my brothers. And oh, what a dream it was. I saw what King Nebuchadnezzar saw when he dreamed and God gave me the meaning. I will tell you all about it soon, but first we must leave."

"Leave?" Shadrach questioned. "But where are we going, Daniel?"

"You've been promoted. All three of you!"

I thought that my lack of food from the fast we had endured since the previous evening was playing tricks with my hearing. I thought Daniel said we had been promoted but I knew this was impossible. Until Daniel went on.

"The king was overjoyed at the interpretation of the dream I brought to him. He now knows that the God of Israel is not only the God of Israel but of all the world. He has appointed me, Daniel, to serve directly in his court. I am to be chief prefect over all the wise men of Babylon as well as the king's assistant over the whole province."

We could only stare at Daniel. Stunned.

How is it, that a Jewish captive from Israel is now managing the affairs of the Black Wind? I had not thought of that phrase in a long time now. The Black Wind. That was because, I realized in that moment, something had changed. In fact, it had been changing for some time. *I* had been changing. Not in a corrupt or compromising way. No, something deeply spiritual was happening in me. In all of us.

I had always been taught that Yahweh was the God of Israel. That all the other peoples of other nations were pagan and hopeless. But I was beginning to consider the notion: *God cares about all people.*

All people.

Even the Babylonians.

It's still not completely clear to me and I must think on this more.

"And that is not all, my brothers." Daniel went on. "The king asked if I had any wishes he could grant. And I could only think of one wish in that moment. I told him he could trust you three just as he now trusts me. And with that, he has promoted you as well. The three of you will be making a new home in the political district. You are to each be given authority over various affairs of the province."

Again, we stared with eyes wide and mouths open.

"We're not going to see you anymore, are we Daniel?" It was Abednego that finally asked the question.

A crease of sadness clouded the twinkle in Daniel's eye. "Most likely not as often. That is true. I will be close to the king each day. But do not worry, there will be times that we can still gather. But just not as frequently."

We all embraced one another with hugs and tears. It was hard to imagine life in Babylon without Daniel's daily presence and words of wisdom.

Pulling from our embrace, Daniel extolled, "Be of good cheer, brothers. I told you some time ago that God was up to something. And I think that this is just the beginning!"

A private entry in the Journal of Meshach
Eleventh day of Šabatu, the third year of the reign of King
Nebuchadnezzar of Babylon
601 B.C.

-16-

I received my first lesson in politics today.

No one is pro*moted unless someone else is* de*moted.*

In my case, that person is a man named Chalda. He *was* the chief historian of Babylon. And now, it appears, that I am the chief historian of Babylon. I feel fiercely underqualified for such a position, but Captain Arioch assures me that Chalda has struggled to find favor with the king's counsel and even the king himself. This is actually better for Chalda, for it removes him from a spotlight under which he has been wilting.

But I don't think Chalda sees it that way.

"Filthy Jew!" is what I heard him exclaim under his breath as I was introduced as his new superior. He threw down the quill he was holding and summarily marched away.

Shadrach and Abednego are in a better position. Shadrach has been given charge over distribution of the king's grain to the poor. His predecessor has, himself, been promoted so there is no ill will. Abednego is now overseer of domestic trade within the empire. The man he is replacing has apparently been sent into exile to some unknown part of the realm. It seems there are accusations that he was taking personal profit from his position.

The three of us share a new home and we spent the evening settling in.

I am about to lay my head down. It has been a long day. I plan to spend tomorrow familiarizing myself with the history of Babylon.

A private entry in the Journal of Meshach
Twelfth day of Šabatu, the third year of the reign of King
Nebuchadnezzar of Babylon
601 B.C.

-17-

Tomorrow is dedication day.

I've not seen the city of Babylon in such a festive mood as this. King Nebuchadnezzar has ordered the entire population of the city to the Plain of Dura for a ceremony of dedication to the massive statue of himself. After nearly a year, it appears the thing is finally completed.

"It's ugly, I tell you!" Abednego laughed at his own declaration. "I was down there not two weeks ago when it was nearly done. Looks nothing like Nebuchadnezzar at all. Looks more like...Ashpenaz!" He scrunched his face into a sour scowl.

Shadrach joined the fun and threw a pillow across the room at him. "I don't care how ugly it is or if it shines like the Queen of Sheba herself. Do you know how many people could be fed with the gold that has been used to overlay the image? I hear the thing is more than ninety feet tall."

"You're always thinking about feeding the hungry." Abednego threw the pillow back at him.

"Well, it *is* my job. I still can't believe that I, Shadrach - formerly known as Hananiah - a Jew, work for the King of Babylon." He shook his head.

"You speak truth. We all *work* for Nebuchadnezzar but that does not mean we have to *worship* Nebuchadnezzar. I hear talk that he's going to require everyone who attends to bow down and worship the ugly beast."

"Well, this is one Jew who won't be bowing, I can assure you," I chimed in.

"A second from me," came Abednego.

"And me as well," finished Shadrach.

"Don't worry about food for the poor, though," Abednego directed at Shadrach. "I can tell you that the king has opened his storehouses and declared a week of festival after the dedication. He's slaughtering over a thousand head of bull from his private herds and ordering sides of beef distributed to all. No one will be worried about grain when they can have steak. I've seen the books myself. The gold used on that statue of his is a small thing compared to the wealth flowing into the empire from those Nebuchadnezzar continues to conquer."

I thought about Jerusalem at Abednego's words. I thought about the gold vessels from the Temple in Jerusalem that he ordered taken when he selected us for exile nearly four years ago now. Sadness swept over me. A sadness I had not known in a long time. It made me think about my lost family. My mother and father and sister. I wondered how they were doing. Would they eat steak this week? Do they even have enough grain for bread?

Abednego was right. Sometimes in life one may find oneself working for Nebuchadnezzar, but that doesn't mean one has to worship Nebuchadnezzar.

A private entry in the Journal of Meshach
Twenty-first day of Samnu, the fourth year of the reign of King Nebuchadnezzar of Babylon
600 B.C.

-18-

The words I am about to write will sound fantastic. Unbelievable. Whoever may read this will find themselves pressed to accept the truth herein. But, upon my life, true these words are. There are witnesses. The whole of the city surely knows, for they all saw. But I must write it all down, for I do not want to forget a single detail.

Today, I stood before my king and I stood before my God. And my king stood against my God. And my God humbled my king. The great Nebuchadnezzar. Yes, I told you it was beyond belief. But I am only getting started!

My hand and quill suffer to keep up with my mind as the words pour forth. I have stopped several times already to sniff at the skin on my arm. It still smells of the lavender used in my morning bath. Not of smoke. Or of charred flesh. That in itself is the greatest miracle of all. I should not even be here writing these words.

But I get ahead of myself.

We arose early for the march to the Plain of Dura – Shadrach, Abednego, and myself. The whole city was on the move it seemed. We had hoped to travel with Daniel but were told he is out of the city on the king's business.

It is not a long journey on a normal day but took a bit longer than usual because of the crowds. I first caught sight of the thing while some distance off as the rays of the still-rising sun shimmered off its surface. It is a colossus to be sure. Radiating the glory of a man who thinks he's a god. The parade of people in front of us descending onto the plain looked like ants on the march - the plain also dotted with the still-burning furnaces that had been built on site to smelt the gold for the statue. They were belching their smoke high into the sky. The whole scene made me think of the end of the world.

Because of our position on the king's court, we three were ushered to the front section of the crowd to join others who enjoyed the favor of the Great King. We found ourselves not fifty feet from the statue itself. Its gold frame rose into the sky, blocking the sun from where we stood, but creating a golden halo that caused the thing to shine like divinity itself. I was in awe, I will admit.

A massive stage had been erected to the right side of Nebuchadnezzar's gold statue where the king himself sat on a throne. He looked proud and he looked happy. We were close enough to see the smile on his face and glint in his eye.

A herald of the king – a man in a long flowing robe of gold, scarlet, and purple, whose white beard flowed down to his chest – came forward. He unrolled a large parchment scroll and with an impossibly loud voice read:

You are commanded, O peoples, nations, and languages, that when you hear the sound of the horn, pipe, lyre, trigon, harp, bagpipe, and every kind of music, you are to fall down and worship the golden image that King Nebuchadnezzar has set up. And whoever does not fall down and worship shall immediately be cast into a burning fiery furnace.

It was all pomp and circumstance, we knew. Perfectly fitting the indulgences of this particular king. Abednego, Shadrach, and I looked at each other. Our conversation from last evening pinged in our shared minds:

We may have to work *for Nebuchadnezzar, but that doesn't mean we have to* worship *Nebuchadnezzar.*

We acknowledged one another with a slight nod.

A massive blast of trumpets made me jump. A chorus of musical instruments joined, the sound sweeping from the front of the plain to the back. In the span of but a moment, all the people fell to their knees, heads bowed, arms outstretched toward the image of the gold statue.

All the people except for myself and my two friends.

Shadrach and Abednego stared straight ahead but I dared to look behind me. Yes, it was only us left standing. Even the herald had laid down his parchment and taken the stance of worship toward the golden statue. I watched as Nebuchadnezzar surveyed the crowd. He seemed delighted.

After what seemed an eternity - but I am sure it was only a few minutes - the music stopped and the people rose to their feet. It appeared we had survived the ordeal and I was more than ready to return to my duties in the royal library.

That's when a stir of commotion captured my attention. A small group of people – no more than four or five individuals – scrambled onto the stage but were stopped by the king's guard. An animated discussion ensued.

Nebuchadnezzar did not seem pleased at all by this unplanned interruption. There were shouts as arms flailed and then I recognized the leader of the group: Chalda. The man I had unceremoniously replaced as chief librarian for the king.

He was pointing at me, a mask of fury covering his face.

The heads of the king's guard also turned in my direction. The king approached the gathering seeking an explanation, but I already knew.

The king barked some command and his guard clambered down the steps of the stage. The crowd parted like the Red Sea, right to the point where we stood. We did not fight as we were seized and escorted onto the stage to stand in front of the king. I caught Chalda's vicious smile as we were hauled past him.

We had garnered favor with Nebuchadnezzar by way of Daniel some months ago and I could tell the king was struggling with the situation we had created for him.

He approached us and spoke in a surprisingly soft tone. "Shadrach, Meshach, Abednego. What is this thing reported to me? You refuse the order of your king? My order? To serve my gods and to worship the golden image I have created? Surely this is not true."

I was the one who spoke. Not because I am overly courageous. Certainly not. But in that moment, the words I needed to say seemed to come to me with great clarity. There was no hesitation. "It is a true report, Oh Great King. We worship our God, the one true and living God. We cannot worship another."

The king chuckled. "Yes, yes. There are many gods in Babylon. I understand only a little of your God, the God of Israel. But where was he when I came for Jerusalem? Where was he when I took his precious instruments from his Temple?" And then the king's voice took a darker tone. "Where was he to save you when I took you from your families?" He paused to let us think on his question. "This is a small thing, boys. Let the music play and bow to the image. If not, then I must cast you into the furnace of fire, for I have already declared it so. And where will your God be then? Will he rescue you? I think we all know the answer to that question."

Never in my life did I ever imagine that I would stand before the king of the entire world. The only king I had ever known was Jehoiakim, and he was a soft king. But there I was, standing before King Nebuchadnezzar, the greatest king of the greatest empire in all the earth.

Me.

Meshach.

Before Nebuchadnezzar.

I did not so much as cower. And the words that came from my mouth stunned even me.

"Oh Great King Nebuchadnezzar. There is no more for us to say. We cannot bow. If we are to go into the furnace of fire, then so be it. Our God whom we serve is able to deliver us. He is that great! But if not...."

Those three words caused me to pause. Even now, in the writing of this account, they do so again.

But if not...

I am a man of faith. I worship Yahweh, the God of my ancestors, Abraham, Isaac, and Jacob. Yahweh is the one true and living God. The creator of the heavens and the earth. What he created he can manipulate, like clay in the hands of the potter. My whole life I have heard the stories. Of how God delivered our people out from under the hand of Pharaoh of Egypt. Wasn't he the greatest king of the greatest empire in all the earth back then? And what was that to my God? He sent the plagues, the final one of which humbled Pharaoh himself – the plague of the death of the firstborn in the land. God defied the gods of nature and parted the waters of the Red Sea when Pharaoh came for God's people. My God brought manna from the earth and water from a rock. He even stopped the sun in the sky for Joshua in the Valley of Aijalon.

Yes, my God did all of this and I knew my God could save us. But I also know that Yahweh sometimes chooses not to save. My ancestors were slaves in Egypt for four hundred years before Moses came to deliver them, after all. And how many battles did my ancestors lose as they fought to keep the Promised Land? So God, for reasons only God knows, sometimes does not choose to save. But he is still God. And I will still worship him. And that is what I told Nebuchadnezzar, as we stood in the shadow of the pagan beast he had created.

"*But if not*, Oh Great King. If my God does not save us from the furnace of fire, we will still not worship and serve your gods, for we can only worship Yahweh."

And with that, I had no more to say. I had sealed our fate.

The king exploded in fury. With the rage of a bull and spittle flying past his lips, he ordered the furnace closest to the gold statute to be heated seven times its normal temperature. We were dragged from the stage and bound by rope, our hands behind our backs. The crowd was worked into a frenzy, shouting and screaming at the coming sacrifice of fire.

Shadrach began to weep.

"I am sorry," I whispered.

"Do not apologize," he chastised me. "You spoke the truth for us all."

Abednego stood bravely and nodded his head in agreement.

It was settled. We had come to Babylon together and we would now die together.

What came next is something I am still working to sort out in my mind's eye. It feels like a dream, but I know it was not. Three men are dead. That much is true. Burned to death. But not the three men the king expected.

The furnace itself was massive in size, the shape of a tall clay jar, the kind that might contain goat's milk. It bellowed its black smoke into the air, having been stoked to beyond the capacity intended. The heat from the chamber of death was intense as we stood in front of it, its doors closed awaiting the moment they'd be opened and we'd be thrown to our fate.

The trumpets blasted once again and the orchestra of musicians joined in as they had before. The people fell to their faces in worship of the golden image and in that moment the doors of the furnace were pulled wide by men with giant forceps who stood clear of the flames that leapt forth from the terrible maw of the opening.

Like a flash we were covered in light and flame. I heard the screams of the dying. Oh, how horrible it was and my ears still carry the echo of agony. Shadrach, Abednego, and I were propelled forward and we found ourselves on the floor of the furnace. It was in that moment I realized it was not me or either of my friends who had been swallowed by the flames, but instead the poor souls who had bound us and pushed us into the furnace. I looked back and could see their bodies writhing on the ground. No one dared come to their aid for threat of the flames which continued to pour from the furnace's opening.

Confusion.

I felt no pain at all. In fact, I felt no heat save a gentle warmth - the kind one feels on a cold winter night after coming inside to the toasty comfort of a few logs crackling on the hearth. I stood to my feet and that was when I realized my hands were no longer bound. Shadrach and Abednego were also standing. We looked at one another, and not knowing what else to do, embraced one another.

And that was when we saw *him*. Actually, Abednego saw him first. I saw my friend's head turn and I merely followed suit.

His body shown brighter than the sun. But it was not because of the fire. He did not burn. He simply...glowed.

"Oh. My. God." I uttered.

"YES. I AM."

We fell to our knees. Not before a golden image, but before the Creator and sustainer of life. I wept tears of joy.

I knew.

I simply knew that this was Yahweh come to rescue us. I had prepared myself to meet my Maker this day. I just had never imagined it would be in this way.

I felt a bolt of fire shoot through my shoulder, down through my body, and out my feet. Not from the flames of the furnace, but from the touch of the Master. His hand touched me and I knew he wanted me to rise. I stood to my feet, and a face I cannot even begin to describe because I truly have no recollection of it, smiled back at me. That is all I can remember.

The smile of God.

At me.

I could have died in that moment and I would have been content with the life I had lived. But I knew that God had more for me to do.

"Shadrach, Meshach, Abednego!" The voice of King Nebuchadnezzar broke me from my trance. When I looked back *he* was gone. Vanished to heaven from where he had come. The king continued, "Servants of the Most High God. Come to me at once!"

We joined hands and emerged from the furnace of fire. The doors were quickly closed and we eased past three charred bodies - men who had lost their lives while trying to take ours.

"Come stand before me," the king commanded.

We were immediately surrounded. Satraps, prefects, governors, and all the wise men of the king were pressed in close, pulling on our clothes, sniffing at the hairs of our head. Not a whiff of smoke was about us, I knew.

It was a miracle witnessed by the whole of the empire.

King Nebuchadnezzar stared at us in awe. I will never forget that look. The look of sheer power and arrogance, humbled by the hand of the Almighty God of creation.

And then he spoke. "Blessed be the God of Shadrach, Meshach, and Abednego, who has sent his angel and delivered his servants who trusted in him, and set aside the king's command, and yielded up their bodies rather than serve and worship any god except their own God."

What came next was even more stunning. He summoned his herald and the two conferred. There was a lot of hasty scribbling on parchment and then the herald called out for a second time this day:

A decree from King Nebuchadnezzar the Great. Let all who hear obey the words of the Great King. Any people, nation, or language that speaks anything against the God of Shadrach, Meshach, and Abednego shall be torn limb from limb, and their houses laid in ruins, for there is no other God who is able to rescue in this way.

I am alive!

I am more than alive.

The God of heaven and earth saved me today. And not just for today. But for tomorrow and perhaps the day after. And so, as this day ends, and I put my quill away, let these words of mine be a testimony to the greatness of my God. A greatness that can humble even a king.

My shoulder still carries the burn of his touch. I had thought to apply a balm but I think I would rather not. It is a reminder that it was not a dream. Hopefully it will still be burning tomorrow when I awake.

A private entry in the Journal of Meshach
Twenty-second day of Samnu, the fourth year of the reign of King
Nebuchadnezzar of Babylon
600 B.C.

-19-

I have been promoted. Again.

It has not been two days since the miracle in the furnace of fire on the Plain of Dura. The morning began as it usually does, ordinary and non-eventful except I am alive. I still cannot believe it.

Breakfast with Shadrach and Abednego was interrupted by the arrival of Captain Arioch of the king's guard with Ashpenaz the chief of the eunuchs at his side.

They had come for me.

Fear struck like lightning. Had Nebuchadnezzar changed his mind? Was he to throw me back in the furnace a second time? To finish the job he had started only two days previous?

"Gather your things, Meshach. The king requires your service," the captain explained.

The look of confusion on my face must have been telling. *Requires my service?* What did that mean?

Ashpenaz laughed as he offered, "It's a good thing Meshach. The Great King has need of you. He won't quit talking about your survival in the furnace at Dura. I don't know what sort of magic you and your friends conjured but it has cast its spell over the king. It's all he is talking about. He knows you are good with words and at writing. He has promoted you to royal court recorder for the king."

I looked at Shadrach and Abednego. Frozen. Shadrach only lifted his shoulders while Abednego was grinning from ear to ear.

"So, this means...?"

"It means we need to go now!" Ashpenaz was growing impatient. "It means you will be relocated to the royal palace itself where you will live and work in the shadow of the king himself. You will sit in on all sessions of the court as well as all of the Great King's meetings with his generals and advisors. You will travel where the king travels and your sole responsibility is to record all of it for the historical archives of the empire. You will literally be writing history Meshach. Now come! Captain Arioch will help you gather your belongings. Say good-bye to your friends. You may not see them again."

I was stunned. Tears began to flow and I hugged my two best friends. Ashpenaz only rolled his eyes at our show of emotion. Was it true I would never see them again? And I was now the royal court recorder? For the king? For the empire? It was all too much.

I said my good-byes and hastened to collect my things.

"We will be praying for you," shouted Abednego as I left through the doorway of our shared house.

"Say hello to Daniel for us," Shadrach followed with enthusiasm.

Daniel. I had not thought of Daniel. I am leaving two friends behind, but another old friend is waiting for me in my new service to the king.

A private entry in the Journal of Meshach
Twenty-fourth day of Samnu, the fourth year of the reign of King
Nebuchadnezzar of Babylon
600 B.C.

-20-

The Great King Nebuchadnezzar is furious. Word has reached his ears that King Jehoiakim of Judah has rebelled against the king's hand. He has returned his allegiance back to Egypt and has stopped the paying of the royal tribute to the empire. In addition, he has expelled the king's guard from the land of Judah and reports also indicate that he has executed the Great King's generals who were left in charge to manage the king's affairs. We are told that King Jehoiakim went as far as to hang their bodies from the wall of Jerusalem as a final insult to King Nebuchadnezzar.

I have not seen the Great King this angry. Ever. Not in these last two years I have been in his service.

He ordered his army to march immediately for Judah with the king, himself, leading the way.

We have been on the road now for three days and the king has ordered the march to Jerusalem to be completed with haste. Eight months is the goal I am told.

"We will drive hard to the walls of Jerusalem, and then we will drive Jehoiakim from power!" This was the king's declaration.

From the Journal of Meshach, royal court recorder for the king
Second day of Nisānu, the sixth year of the reign of King
Nebuchadnezzar of Babylon
598 B.C.

-21-

I am going home!

How is this possible? That I, Meshach of Babylon, formerly Mishael of Judah, am returning to my homeland? It has been so long since I have thought of myself as Mishael. I left that name behind years ago. But oh, how things have changed.

Yes, I am going home, but not in any way I would ever have imagined. I am riding *with* the Black Wind this time. The conflict I have inside of myself is about to consume me. I have thoughts of my parents and sister. They have no idea of the horror that is coming their way. Oh, how I wish I could warn them. They need to flee the city now. They need to run to the hill country of Galilee. Yes, that would be a good place. I wonder if it will be possible to get word to them before the siege begins. I don't see how, though.

Jehoiakim has pushed King Nebuchadnezzar too far this time. There is no hope for him, and I fear for the population of Jerusalem.

I am going home. And I will discharge my duty, writing down an accurate account of the judgement that Nebuchadnezzar will issue from his mighty hand. What more can I do? I will write, because that is my job. And I will pray because that is my devotion.

"Lord, God of heaven and earth, I pray for the peace of Jerusalem."

A private entry in the Journal of Meshach
Second day of Nisānu, the sixth year of the reign of King
Nebuchadnezzar of Babylon
598 B.C.

-22-

The siege of Jerusalem has begun.

My heart soared as we crested Mount Olivet and the Temple came into view just across the valley, surrounded by the great walls of the city. And then my heart sank as I knew what was coming next for the city that had once been my home.

Shadrach is here with me. What a pleasant surprise, when two months into the journey, we found one another. Once Shadrach became aware that King Nebuchadnezzar had ordered a march on Israel, he leveraged his position and gained permission to join the troupe. His job is to oversee the food supply chain and make sure the army of Babylon is well fed while on campaign.

Together we stood on Olivet and wept for Jerusalem.

"I can only think of my family," he said, wiping the tears that flowed with the back of his hand.

I nodded silently in return. Then I spoke. "Yahweh took care of us before. He will take care of them now."

"It's not Yahweh I am concerned about, Meshach. It's Nebuchadnezzar. His wrath knows no end. He is done with King Jehoiakim and his rebellious ways. Look at the Temple."

He pointed toward the Temple Mount. "Where is the smoke that should be flowing from the altar? Where is the scent of burning animal flesh that should be in the air? The sacrifices have ceased. And the Temple itself looks to be in poor condition. It's difficult to tell from this distance, but it looks to need a good cleaning. Not only has Jehoiakim rebelled against Nebuchadnezzar, he's rebelled against Yahweh. Perhaps you are right." He turned and looked at me. "Perhaps Yahweh *will* take care of Jehoiakim. Just not in the way you meant. And when he does...what then of our families? They will likely be caught in the wake of the wrath of both a king *and* God."

Shadrach was right. And I wept even more.

A private entry in the Journal of Meshach

Fourth day of Kislimu, the seventh year of the reign of King Nebuchadnezzar of Babylon

598 B.C.

-23-

The siege is over.

It took just over ninety days, or three months, but Jehoiakim is no more. I am glad it was quick, for much of the city was spared.

I've been able to do nothing but watch and keep the official record of the siege. There has been little to do and even less to write, really.

The end came all of a sudden and took us by surprise.

The Lion Gate was opened at dawn. From the inside. It seems King Nebuchadnezzar was not the only one done with Jehoiakim. The army poured in and Nebuchadnezzar was summoned from his tent once the city was secured.

The king had no desire to enter the city directly. He simply ordered that Jehoiakim be brought to him. An hour later, Jehoiakim was on his knees in chains before

Nebuchadnezzar as the Great King causally ate his breakfast. I was standing only feet behind Nebuchadnezzar as Jehoiakim pleaded for his life. It was a pitiful sight indeed.

King Nebuchadnezzar ignored the wailing of the man until he'd finished his pork cut, fruit, and cake. He washed it all down with a large cup of wine, wiped his mouth with a cloth from the small table, and then rose to his feet. The king drew in a long, slow breath and then...like a hammer of thunder erupting from a storm cloud, he launched the breakfast table to the side with a mighty toss of his arm. He strode the short distance to Jehoiakim, screaming only the name of the captain of his guard.

"Rihat!" he bellowed.

And as if the whole thing had been choreographed in advance, Rihat tossed a battle sword to the king. Nebuchadnezzar caught the four-foot blade by the hilt and in one fluid motion lopped off the head of Jehoiakim. I looked on in stunned silence as did all of us gathered around. Jehoiakim's head rolled off the right shoulder of his body and came to rest, eyes wide open, as if staring up at the Great King in wonder. His body pitched forward onto the ground, gushing its red content onto the ground from the neck. Any desire to partake of my own breakfast was lost.

Just like that, it was over.

"Let his son take his place as ruler over this cursed city. What is his name again?"

"Jehoiachin, Oh Great King," Captain Rihat replied.

"Jehoia*chin*, you say. Son of Jehoia*kim*."

"Yes, your majesty. That is correct."

King Nebuchadnezzar only grinned as if the similarity in names was humorous to him. "Deliver Jehoia*kim's* head to his son. Jehoia*chin*." He placed emphasis on the last syllable of each name. "Hang the body from the city walls. And let's see if the son can behave himself better than the father."

And with that, King Nebuchadnezzar ordered half of the army back to Babylon, and half to stay and make sure there was no more rebellion.

Tomorrow, it is back to Babylon we go.

From the Journal of Meshach, royal court recorder for the king
Thirtieth day of Adār, the seventh year of the reign of King
Nebuchadnezzar of Babylon
598 B.C.

-24-

The son did no better than the father. In fact, he did worse.

The reign of King Jehoiachin lasted three months and ten days. No sooner had we departed for Babylon than did King Nebuchadnezzar receive word that Jehoiachin had inherited his father's rebellious ways. Whatever lesson the Great King had intended to teach by the beheading of Jehoiakim, it had not been learned.

I was present in the tent when King Nebuchadnezzar gave the orders.

"I am weary of this rabble of Hebrew people in Israel. I have tried, over and over it seems, to be a benevolent ruler to a people who know only rebellion." The Great King actually looked tired as he slumped his shoulders. Then his resolve returned. "Captain Rihat, I want you to take the city. Maybe someone will betray this son of a king and open the gates for us again, but if not, lay siege and starve them out if you have to. Once inside, strip that precious Temple of theirs." The thunder of his voice had returned. "Take it all! The gold, the silver, the bronze. Take every sacred thing from that wicked Temple and bring it to me in Babylon. And appoint ten thousand people this time for exile. Including this child, Jehoiachin. I want to see him grovel before me in front of my throne along the Euphrates River. Perhaps stripping the land of its wealth and its people will be enough this time. And find some puppet to make as king over them. Someone soft, that we can control. I don't ever want to come back to this land."

From the Journal of Meshach, royal court recorder for the king
Twenty-third day of Āru, the seventh year of the reign of King
Nebuchadnezzar of Babylon
597 B.C.

-25-

When this day began, I felt so tired. And I felt old.

I am only thirty-three years of age now and yet I feel I have witnessed the best and worst of humanity in that span of time. I've lived over half my life now in Babylon. It is a good life, I must admit. I lack for nothing. My God has protected me from the harsh treatment that most of my fellow Jews endure living as exiles.

There truly is no hope that I will ever return home to the Promised Land of Israel. And I am not even sure I would want to anymore even if I could. The place I once knew is no more.

Zedekiah, the puppet king installed after Jehoiachin, lasted but eleven years and then...another rebellion. This time, the Great King Nebuchadnezzar really had had enough. He ordered the city sacked and razed. The Temple of

Yahweh was burned to the ground and the walls of the Holy City were torn down. In my youth, I would never have thought such a thing possible, but the might and power of the Babylonian Empire knows no match. I have seen it first hand, traveling with the Great King, recording in meticulous detail his exploits. I was there when Nebuchadnezzar ordered that King Zedekiah's sons be slaughtered in front of him for his act of rebellion. And then the Great King himself, gouged out the eyes of Zedekiah using his own thumbs as the wicked tools.

The Great King Nebuchadnezzar has conquered the whole world it seems now. He walks onto the roof of his royal palace each day and takes in the view of all that is his. I was with him two nights ago for such a viewing as he uttered the words, "Is not this great Babylon, which I have built by my mighty power as a royal residence and for the glory of my majesty?"

I think the Great King believes he is now a great god.

After Zedekiah's rebellion was crushed and the city of Jerusalem sacked, forty thousand more of my countrymen were forced into exile and the bulk of my fellow Jews now live along the River Chebar here in Babylon.

I continue to live in luxury in the king's palace. And yes, my soul torments me at times because of this. I have spent much time wondering how it is that Yahweh - my God and the one true and living God - could turn his back on us, his chosen people. How he could allow his Holy Temple to be desecrated and burned by heathens. How he could stand by and do nothing as the Promised Land of Israel dries up into nothing. The milk and honey no longer flow.

But then I think of all the kings. Jehoiakim and his son Jehoiachin. And then Zedekiah. And before these three a countless host of so many others, most of whom – not all but most – rebelled against God and did what was evil in the sight of the Lord. Yes, it is true. In the shadow of the Holy Temple there were altars to other gods. Around the whole Holy City, on every rooftop it seemed, there were even more altars burning incense to the pagan gods of Baal, and Asherah, and Molech. Rephan, Tammuz and countless others. I grew up around these altars. I inhaled the fragrance of the burning incense as I walked the streets of the city, and I thought nothing of it, I admit. But now, years later, separated by time and distance, I can see with different eyes.

Before the kings of Judah rebelled against the Great King of Babylon, they had already rebelled against God. Yahweh saw the altars too. And he smelled the incense as well. Only he didn't ignore this abomination. I imagine that, just like Nebuchadnezzar, Yahweh finally had enough. But rather than unleash the army of heaven and all its angels against his own people, Yahweh chose to do something different. Very different. He chose to give us all what we asked for. If God's people no longer wanted God, then he would give them that. If the Spirit of God was no longer wanted in the land of Israel, then he would simply leave. And that is exactly what I think happened. Yahweh left and along with his leaving also left his protective hand. That is why Nebuchadnezzar was successful in taking the once Holy Land and leaving it in ruins. In the end, God's people got exactly what they wanted. A world without God.

But God is not absent. I learned that lesson a long time ago. His protective hand has been with me and watched over me all these years.

And miracle of miracles! This morning I went for a tour of the Jewish settlement by the River Chebar. I was walking through the encampment of tents and the beginnings of more permanent homes of mud brick and thatched roofing. Everywhere the air was smoke-filled with small fires for cooking and burning refuse. But somehow, through the mass of bleating goats and moving people...I saw her face. A face from so long ago that I had nearly forgotten.

It was Mary!

Mary, daughter of Benjamin and Leah. My mind went back to that last day I had seen her, when the Black Wind had invaded Jerusalem for the first time. She'd been stripped and abused by a horde of Babylonian fiends and I had been helpless to stop it. The shame of that day eighteen years ago flooded back upon my soul.

And then that face found mine. And she smiled.

I am not sure how it happened but in the span of a moment we had found each other and inexplicably she was in my arms and we embraced one another and we wept. These many years later, she still radiates with the beauty of her youth.

"Mishael," she began. "How...how are you here? And look at how you are dressed. You've done much better than the rest of us, I think." Her face glowed and her smile widened. She knew my name! She remembered. I had never had the courage to follow my heart when we were young. I had let station stand between me and Mary. But station meant nothing anymore. We were both Jews, living in exile. It was that simple. But I did have influence.

Before I could answer Mary, her eyes grew wide. "Come quickly. You must follow me, Mishael. It's a miracle. A miracle of Yahweh!" She grabbed my hand and led the way nearly faster than I could keep up. We arrived at a small canvas tent and Mary flung the door aside and pulled me inside. For the second time this day, my eyes fell on another face. My mouth gaped as did the mouth of the other face. Mary beamed, her smile wide.

It was Ruth. My sister.

We embraced and wept and kissed each other's cheeks and wept some more. She was but a child the last time I had seen her. And now she was a woman.

And she was also pregnant.

Morning bled into afternoon as we sat in the little tent, the day becoming a mixture of joy and grief. Mary filled in the missing years for me. My parents are dead. My father was killed during the rebellion of Jehoiakim. I tore my clothes when she told me this. I had been outside the walls of the city that day but knew nothing of the death of my own father. Mother died on the march from Jerusalem to Babylon. She was frail and became sick on the march and departed this earth after two months into the journey. And then Ruth. Brave, dear Ruth. She had married when she came of age. A good man, she explained, named Baruch. He had fought the Babylonian army during the rebellion of Zedekiah and died by the sword. On the march of exiles to Babylon, she'd been raped by a soldier and the result was her swelling belly. Anger. Sadness. Rage. Joy. I would not have thought it possible to experience such a rainbow of emotions all at once.

Mary's parents had perished as well. They had starved to death during the siege of Jehoiachin's rebellion, leaving Mary alone. She had never married.

I made up my mind in that moment to change both of their circumstances. Mary doesn't know it yet, but I intend to marry her. I love her. Yes, it's true. I can't explain it, but seeing her today ignited something in me I thought had disappeared forever. We will marry and she will join me in the royal palace along with my sister Ruth. Ruth will give birth to a baby, and Mary and I will help her raise the child. Yahweh has granted me privilege and influence and I intend to use them for good.

When this day began, I felt so tired. And I felt old.

As this day ends, I feel alive. And I feel young!

A private entry in the Journal of Meshach

Fifth day of the month of Addāru, the eighteenth year of the reign of King Nebuchadnezzar of Babylon
586 B.C.

-26-

The king is sick.

Today marks the fourth month according to the calendar of Babylon. When the illness began, it was thought to be a common drought of mind and body, typically lasting no more than seven to ten days. After the first month the court began to express concern. The king's temperament seemed most affected. Fits of rage and ravings that make no sense to one of sound thought. He resisted any attempt by the royal physicians to provide care and he turned violent, ordering them out of his presence, throwing his golden chamber pot and its contents at them as they fled.

Those he trusts most, his inner circle of advisors, can no longer approach him. He only grunts and raves continually, always growing agitated the longer social contact persists. Even Heabani, the one closest to the king and the most trusted of all, has been cast out. In seeking to faithfully and accurately record the account of the king's illness I have pressed Heabani for details on its origins. He is quite certain it began in the month of Addāru when the moon shone at its fullest. It was on that night that the king returned from his walk along the flat roof of the royal palace, a most favorite location of the king to gaze upon the vastness of his kingdom, especially on this one night with the lights of the heavens showing at their brightest.

"A curse! A CURSE...!" the king yelled as he stormed into his bedchamber. "The gods have unmade me...I am finished!" He's not come out since.

Haebani insists it's a sickness of the moon. I personally believe in no such thing but his moods and temperament do seem to swing like the hammer of a great pendulum as the moon itself wanes and waxes. The height of his ravings always peaking as the moon itself peaks each month. But he always spirals down, never ultimately getting better.

So now, after five long months, it is clear — the king is sick. He is sick in mind, for sure. But he is also sick in body. Five months in his bedchamber, not once coming out to bathe or to freshen his clothing. His hair and beard grow long and matted. He is soiled as is his bedding. The whole room reeks of human waste and rotten food. Some days he eats but many he does not. The chambermaids refuse to attend to him out of fear. Royal guards do what they can to swipe old food and to clean up after the king, but such attempts are always cut short by the king's violence toward all who come near. He is still the king after all.

Everyone in this country worships their own gods and I have mine. Tonight, the priests are coming to burn incense and to offer sacrifices for the king and his healing. They will be praying to their gods for the king's relief, and I will be praying to mine.

From the Journal of Meshach, royal court recorder for the king
Sixth day of the month of Dumuzu, the nineteenth year of the reign of
King Nebuchadnezzar of Babylon
585 B.C.

-27-

Even the Great King is not immune to the curse of the gods it seems.

Nebuchadnezzar has finally been humbled. For three years now he has been lost to us. His wild ravings and uncontrollable and bizarre behavior have relegated him to the royal stockyards where he lives among the animals he once slaughtered for his banquet table.

A pen of sorts was constructed to protect him from the bulls and wild hogs, but honestly, he is so mad and full of impossible strength the pen serves to protect the poor beasts from him. After he eviscerated a young bull with nothing but the unnaturally long nails of his hands and his teeth, the decision to build the enclosure was set.

The Great King looks nothing of his former self. There

is nothing great about him any longer. He is a pitiful thing to behold, indeed.

Very few have access to him. It must be this way. The people of the empire cannot know that their king has fallen to such a place of loathing and ruin. His advisors and those close to him in the royal court are fiercely loyal to him and have done a fine job maintaining the charade that all is well. But all is most certainly not well.

I am one of the few who may see him, not that I choose to do so very often. I am both sad and disgusted when I take the short walk to where he grazes. Yes, that is the word for it. He stalks about on all fours now, grazing on the grass of the fields like an ox.

The Babylonian Empire is at peace with the world, it seems, and that is a good thing. Nebuchadnezzar had conquered all there was to conquer before the curse inflicted his mind and body. His generals roam the empire, easily quelling any uprising that might occur here or there.

For my part, my life is simple and at peace. Mary and I are immensely happy and enjoy the company of my little nephew, Samuel. Ruth is a fine mother and together we are a family. Mary is pregnant now and we look forward to having what would amount to a brother or sister for Samuel to play with soon.

I paid a visit to the king's pen earlier today. It had been months since I'd attended to him in this manner, but as royal recorder of the history of the Babylonian Empire, it is necessary that I at least make note of any change.

Daniel came with me this time. He too, is one of the few who has access to the king. We stood at the wooden fence and stared at the "Great King."

"How is it that a king can be brought to this?" I asked.

"A king is only a man, Meshach. The title of king is only an invention of this world designed to draw lines. To separate some from others. But in the end, we are all the same. We rise, we eat and breathe, and then we lay our heads down at night. And such it is for all people everywhere."

"But this," I said as I leaned on the fence, my elbows propped on the railing and pointed at the beast that was a king. "This is not all people everywhere. This is not like anything I have ever seen before. And I have seen much in my life, Daniel."

We watched as Nebuchadnezzar burrowed into the weeds and dirt with his face. His hair has grown long and is matted and covered in mange. His beard matches, making his face invisible behind a barrier of unkempt filth. He shed his clothes a long time ago and so he prowls around naked. But he does not look like a man anymore. The curse has caused a coat of hair to grow on his body as well. It parts along his boney spine which protrudes unnaturally as it runs the length of his back. His hands and feet have morphed into a form of claw-like paws. He truly is more animal than man now.

"What we see in front of us is the work of God, Meshach. When a man thinks of himself as more than a man, to the point that he takes on the role of God...well, God will have the final word on that, I can assure you. What we are seeing here is the final word of God."

Daniel's words soaked in as the beast-king lifted his head and gazed at us. Was there recognition in those eyes? For a moment I thought it so. But then the creature lifted his head and howled at the sun and went back to the hole he was digging.

From the Journal of Meshach, royal court recorder for the king
Tenth day of the month of Samnu, the twenty-second year of the reign
of King Nebuchadnezzar of Babylon
582 B.C

-28-

The king has returned!

It was a glorious feast last evening in honor of the Great King of Babylon. The festival hall was full of family, advisors, and court officiants. All the king's favorite dishes were served and he ate like an animal, although an animal he is no more. The curse of the last seven years suddenly lifted, and without warning. It has not yet been a full three days since he simply stood up in the outdoor pen that had become his new home, and walked back to the palace. On his own and in his right mind. He was a mess, of course. Filthy and weather-beaten. Nearly unrecognizable because of the length of his hair and beard, but the animal nature that had overtaken him was absent.

I was in the great Hanging Garden, reading and meditating on a portion of the Torah, the Holy Word of my

God from my ancient homeland (it seems like another life, so many years since I called Israel home - Babylon is where I lay my head now and likely will for the rest of my days), when the king himself walked past me. Servants were scurrying at his sudden appearance. Someone had laid a robe over his shoulders to cover his naked form. The king stopped as he passed me, sensing my presence I can only assume. He looked at me with his piercing dark eyes and I knew then that he had returned. Then he said to me the most stunning thing in my native tongue of Hebrew: "Yahweh Shalom." *The Lord is peace.* Never before had I heard the Great King, a man of many gods, invoke the name of my God.

The miracle of his transformation continued at the banquet. For the Great King stood at one moment in the middle of the feast and called the court to his attention. He gave a speech that left all those in attendance without speech:

My kingdom has been restored to me. My majesty and splendor have returned to me. Now I, Nebuchadnezzar, praise and extol and honor the King of Heaven. For all his works are right and his ways are just. Believe me when I declare this truth. Those who walk in pride, he is able to humble.

The Great King of Babylon was speaking about my God! Is it possible that he has become a follower of the one true and living God? Praise be to Yahweh if this be so. Time will tell.

From the Journal of Meshach, royal court recorder for the king
Sixth day of the month of Adār, the twenty-sixth year of the reign of
King Nebuchadnezzar of Babylon
579 B.C.

-29-

I find myself overjoyed and also troubled by the transformation of King Nebuchadnezzar.

Overjoyed that he has been restored. Overjoyed that his bigger-than-life presence will ensure that the peace brought on by his reign will continue. And overjoyed that he gives all the glory for his restoration and return to Yahweh, the God of heaven and earth.

And that, it seems, is also the source of my troubled spirit. How is it possible that God would show mercy and grace upon one such as Nebuchadnezzar? Unable to settle the battle in my soul, I sought out the much wiser Daniel this afternoon. I found him in the Hanging Garden, a place of beauty and serenity like no other, a true wonder of the world that I have taken to enjoying in recent years.

Daniel listened with a calm smile as I articulated the inner conflict raging inside of me.

"You sound like a Jew who doesn't know the Word of God, Meshach," he began with a playful jab toward me. "Or at least a Jew that only knows half of the Word of God."

"What on earth are you talking about, Daniel?" I may have sounded lighthearted in my response, but that only served to conceal the true sense of questioning I felt toward where he was going. "What does my Jewishness and God's Holy Word have to do with God and Nebuchadnezzar? Let me be plain. Here is my struggle. Nebuchadnezzar is the Great King of the Black Wind. The same Black Wind that blew into our homeland twenty-five years ago and stole you and me from our families and our lives. This is the same Nebuchadnezzar that laid siege to God's Holy City on more than one occasion. He starved our people. He raped our people. He murdered our people. He murdered my family, Daniel!" My voice and demeanor changed and I grew louder than I intended. Such talk, if heard by the wrong people, could cause me to lose my head. But then again, that was also part of the problem of Nebuchadnezzar.

I lowered my voice to a whisper and continued. "Nebuchadnezzar sacked the Holy City. He tore down its walls, leaving it defenseless. He stripped the Temple, Daniel. The Holy Temple of Yahweh. He stole all of its vessels and sacrificial instruments of gold and silver and bronze and brought them here, to the storehouses of Babylon. But not before he burned the Temple itself. So tell me, how is it that Yahweh can restore one such as this? How is it that he can justly accept the worship of one such as Nebuchadnezzar?" I ended my rant, having said more than I intended and more than I should have. But the posture of my heart was now clearly exposed.

The smile had fled from Daniel's face. His response was one I will never forget.

"You know the Torah, do you not, Meshach?" he asked and I nodded. "You know the covenant God made with Abraham then?" Again, I nodded. "And God said to Abraham: I have chosen you from out of all the peoples on the earth. I will make your name great, Abraham. And I will make you a great nation. One day, your descendants will number the stars of the sky. And all those who bless you will be blessed and all those who curse you will be cursed."

"Yes, yes, I know the promise." I cut Daniel off. My patience was still thin. "And that's the problem, don't you see? Nebuchadnezzar has cursed Israel. So how is it that

God has failed to curse Babylon? It seems to me that instead he has blessed this land, and Nebuchadnezzar in particular."

"No, Meshach! Don't *you* see?" It was the first time Daniel had ever raised his voice to me. "A Jew knowing only half of God's Word. I said it once and I say it now a second time. The covenant of God with Abraham. I go back to that because you cut me off before I could finish. The last part is the most important part. God chose Abraham and his descendants to be a special people. And so we are, the Jewish people. Very special to God. But our people are only the beginning of a greater covenant God has planned for *all people*. Don't you know the last part of the covenant with Abraham?" He paused and I stared. "Here let me remind you. God said to Abraham: Behold one day, through you, *all the people of the earth* will be blessed.

"Please tell me you see it, Meshach. It is so important that you see and understand. The last part of the covenant is the key to the whole thing. God never chose us as Jews just so he could have us and keep us. No. He chose us so that *through us*, the whole world could come to know and worship Yahweh. The prophets speak of one who is coming, a prince of peace, who will establish this covenant with all people, not just us Jews. This prince of peace is yet to come, but the covenant with Abraham has already revealed the heart of God. He loves all people, Meshach. All people, everywhere. It was never about only the Jews. It was always about every nation and tribe. For God so loves the *whole* world. Why then is it so hard to believe, that a God who loves the Jews - even when we reject him, and build altars to other gods, and burn incense and offer sacrifices to other gods - couldn't also love the people of Babylon...and also her king? Especially, when that king humbles himself and surrenders himself and worships Yahweh as the one true and living God.

"You see, Meshach? Please tell me you see. God can love anybody. God can *forgive* anybody. Even a pagan king."

He was right, of course. Daniel is always right it seems.

"You may not like it," he continued, sensing my hesitancy. "But you must accept it. And what would truly be wonderful is if you and I prayed for Nebuchadnezzar. That God would keep him humble and keep him soft. Imagine the impact a king like Nebuchadnezzar could have should he stay under the hand of God."

And that is what we did before leaving the Hanging Garden. We prayed.

Jeffrey S. Crawford

A private entry in the Journal of Meshach
Fourteenth day of the month of Adār, the twenty-sixth year of the reign
of King Nebuchadnezzar of Babylon
579 B.C.

-30-

These are difficult days.

Or I suppose I should say that these are difficult years. Not since my youth, living in Jerusalem under threat of a Babylonian invasion, have I felt the anxiety of an entire city as I do now.

To say that Nebuchadnezzar is missed would be an understatement. And it is difficult to believe that I have actually penned those words: *Nebuchadnezzar is missed.* Never would I have thought such a thing possible when his name first came to my ears when I was but fifteen years old.

Now my years number sixty-four and I have seen much life, death, war, peace, and yes...treachery. The last six years have been marked by unprecedented turmoil in the empire. Little did we know, upon Nebuchadnezzar's death, what was to follow.

I still remember the day of his royal funeral like it was yesterday. The whole of the empire, it seems, was there on the Plain of Dura for the occasion. I will admit I wept tears of sorrow as did the company of my friends: Shadrach, Abednego, and Daniel. We all stood there for the ceremony and then we followed as his sarcophagus was carried to its tomb. The Great King was now set for his final journey to Irkallu, The Great Below. We all understood that things were about to change.

Nebuchadnezzar's son, Amel-Marduk, ruled well enough. But even then, rumblings that the Medes were on the move could be heard. So many of them were immigrating to Babylon in those days, and their numbers created problems for the governors of the districts where they settled.

Then came the usurper. Neriglissar used his influence as Nebuchadnezzar's son-in-law to infiltrate the highest levels of influence, and then he turned on the family. I will admit that I failed my king. I was only beginning to put the pieces together when the assassin slit Amel-Marduk's throat while he slept next to his wife.

The usurper became king and that was the day the kingdom changed. Peace was no more. A sense of trouble has dominated the city of Babylon that carries even to today.

There is a saying that what one sows, one will also reap. It was only four years and then Neriglissar died under "mysterious circumstances." I suppose that is the kind way of saying that his death was not natural. Royal succession demanded his son assume the throne, which he did. But Labashi-Marduk was but a boy when he did so, and completely unfit for rule. He was also a brat of a child. Serving him was most unpleasant.

Clearly the empire was in jeopardy and those in the highest places of the court recognized this. And so entered Nabonidus, along with his son, Belshazzar, who hatched their own conspiracy to dispose of the boy. Were the young man not so nasty, I would almost have been sad.

We are now left with Belshazzar. Co-regent and functioning King of Babylon. His father is on a mission to replace the gods of Babylon with his own god. The god, Marduk, has been demoted, and Nabonidus's preferred god, Sin, has replaced him. I can tell you the priests are unhappy, as is the majority of the population. Nabonidus has left the city on a campaign to build temples to Sin all across the empire. That has left Belshazzar fully in control.

I will serve Belshazzar, just as I have served his predecessors. All kings drink to excess, but this one drinks beyond excess. Too much, by my estimation.

Not only do I feel old, but I *am* old.

Yesterday, it was Nebuchadnezzar and the god, Marduk. Today, it is Belshazzar and the god, Sin. But through it all, it has always been my God Yahweh who has been faithful and true. And it is to him, no other god or king, that I will bow.

A private entry in the Journal of Meshach
Tenth day of the month of Ulūlu, the first year of the reign of King Belshazzar of Babylon
556 B.C.

-31-

The king has lost his mind.

Not in the same way as the Great King Nebuchadnezzar those many years ago, but then again, Belshazzar is not Nebuchadnezzar. He is a fool king who has surrounded himself with fool advisors. The city is being marched upon. The dread of the Medes and the Persians is coming to us here. Soon the city will be sieged, I fear, and then there will be no escape.

Thankfully, not all in the royal court are as delusional as the king. We've all heard the stories of what the Medes and the Persians are capable of. There will be rape and murder. The city will be plundered for its wealth. No one will be spared, including the king's family - especially the king's family. I have lived this before. When Nebuchadnezzar himself, with the power of Babylon, marched on my home -

the beloved city of Jerusalem. Nebuchadnezzar was a ruthless warrior. Many in the royal family were murdered, and the rest of us - the young ones - were taken. I am thankful to my God that I found favor in the eyes of the Great King. He softened after the period of the curse and finished his reign with dignity.

Belshazzar has no dignity. He drinks until he is drunk. Mighty Babylon has already fallen. He just does not know it. It will soon be the footstool of Persia. Another trophy in the beast's march across the world. Even now the king plans a party for all his fool friends for the night after next. By then, the Medes and Persians will be on our doorstep.

There must be action now. We can wait no longer. I was a young man when Babylon came for my family. But now my years are expanded, having reached the mark of eighty. My strength is not as it was, but what strength I have left I will use to serve the king even though he knows it not.

Arrangements have been made. Thankfully, others see the folly of this king and have listened to my counsel. They know my story. They know what awaits those who are of royalty when they are conquered by their foes. All has been done quietly and with many whispers, but when the time comes, members of the royal family will leave. It will be an

.

exodus of another kind. Not by force but by choice. May Yahweh guide them and lead them and grant them favor. Even though they don't know my God, my God knows them. And loves them. My God loves all the peoples of the earth.

I doubt the king will come to his senses and go with them. He will likely die with a drink in his hand.

For my part, I will stay. The family has asked me to journey with them, but I am too old. Mary is dead now and buried here in Babylon and I will join her soon enough. I tried to send my son, Malphious, and his family, but he refuses to leave. I've warned him of the brutality of an invading army but he is unpersuaded. So, we will stay and face the ravages of yet another world empire.

From the Journal of Meshach, royal court recorder for the king
Twenty-fourth day of the month of Tišritum, the fourteenth year of
reign of King Belshazzar of Babylon
539 B.C.

-32-

"Daniel, Daniel! Have you heard? The king has issued a decree. The impossible has become possible!"

I ran as fast as my old legs would carry me to Daniel's quarters this afternoon. The decree of Cyrus the Great has changed the future of my people. I found my aged friend in the upper chamber of his house. His windows were open to the West, toward Jerusalem, and he was on his knees praying.

I stopped short at the sight. "I am so sorry to disturb you, Daniel. Please, forgive me. I will wait outside."

"It is not necessary," he strained to say as he pulled himself upright. There were tears in his eyes. He had heard the news as well.

"It is a miracle, Daniel!" My enthusiasm returned.

"Yes, it is a miracle." There was a quiver of excitement in his voice as well. We made our way to the porch and

Daniel motioned for me to take a seat in one of the cushioned chairs. He found his own seat next to mine.

"Cyrus the Great truly is great," I exclaimed. "I had not expected such deference toward the Jewish population. Especially not from a pagan king who has so recently conquered the Babylonians."

The first days of the Medo-Persian invasion had been harsh, indeed. It was an invasion after all. And as was foreseen, King Belshazzar had been savagely killed once the city walls were breached. He'd been summarily removed from the throne and his head had been summarily removed from his shoulders. And just like that, the Babylonian Empire was no more. We had been successful in spiriting the better part of the royal family out of the city. The new king had made no attempt to pursue them. Within days we saw quickly that Cyrus would be a different kind of king and that Persia would be a different kind of empire.

But none of us expected the decree that Cyrus the Great issued early this morning. I hastened to write the words down so I would never forget them:

Thus says Cyrus king of Persia: The Lord, the God of heaven, has given me all the kingdoms of the earth, and he has charged me to build him a house at Jerusalem, which is in Judah. Whoever is among you of all his people, may his God be with him, and let him go up to Jerusalem, which is in Judah, and rebuild the house of the Lord, the God of Israel—he is the God who is in Jerusalem. And let each survivor, in whatever place he sojourns, be assisted by the men of his place with silver and gold, with goods and with beasts, besides freewill offerings for the house of God that is in Jerusalem.

"Why are you so surprised, my young friend?" Daniel asked with a twinkle in those brown eyes of his, now surrounded by wrinkled skin. Although I am eighty years old, and Daniel still bests me by two years, we've taken up a manner of humor in our advanced age. He calls me "young friend" and I call him "old friend." My old friend continued on with his chastisement of me. "You should know better by now, Meshach. Yahweh holds the heart of any king in his hand. He can do with it as he wishes. He can mold it to the form that suits him. Are you so old now that you've forgotten the miracle of Nebuchadnezzar? Why is it so impossible to believe that God has not directed the King of Persia to send our people back home? And after seventy years *exactly*. Just as that crazy old prophet, Jeremiah, said all those years ago. God is only keeping his word." Daniel laughed.

I laughed as well. "And not just return home, but Cyrus the Great has ordered the rebuilding of God's Holy Temple. *And* he's commanded the people of the land to hand over the gold and silver to do it with. Amazing."

"Amazing *God*."

"I so wish Shadrach and Abednego could be here to see this." I thought of our two friends - brothers really. We had traveled so far together, seen so much together. But they are both sleeping with our fathers now, in their eternal rest.

"They know," Daniel replied. "They can see from where they are now."

We sat in silence, contemplating the grandeur of the moment. The sky was blue and a cool breeze wafted across the porch. I could hear children playing in the streets below. It was a joyous day.

I finally spoke, saying the words that we both were thinking. "We're not going back, are we Daniel?"

He smiled, as he always does. I've lost count of how many times I've seen his lips curl in that fashion.

"No. I don't believe we are," was his answer. And we sat in silence for another bit longer.

It is too far for a couple of old men. Our time has passed. I will send my family, of course. Malphious will protest in the same way he had when I mentioned leaving with the exodus of the royal family. But this is different. This is about Jerusalem. And we are Jews. It is time to go home. For them. Not for me or for Daniel. My old friend never married and so he has no family. But he has me. We will stay together...in Babylon...now part of the Persian Empire. And we will see what other miracles will issue forth from this new king.

A private entry in the Journal of Meshach
First day of the month of Kislimu, the first year of the reign of Cyrus the Great of Persia
539 B.C.

-33-

"What do you know of this Darius?"

I was back at Daniel's home for lunch today. We were discussing the newly installed king of the Babylonian province of the Persian Empire. Cyrus the Great has more land to conquer and greater concerns than a now subdued Babylonia. We received word last month that Darius the Mede was being sent to rule the land by proxy for Cyrus the Great.

"Well, my young friend, he's only been here a week," he chided me in his playful way. "There is not much to know as of yet, but so far so good. I think I like him."

"I was able to gain a short audience with him yesterday. He wanted to meet Belshazzar's attendants and the palace guard. I was amazed when he retained us all. I am still the royal court recorder, it seems. Not that I mind but I am sure he can find someone younger to carry the task if he so desires."

"A wise man does not pull the strings of change unnecessarily. And when he does pull them, a wise man considers the timing of such change. Many times, it is not about *if* but *when*." Daniel let me contemplate his words for a moment before he finished. "I judge Darius to be a wise man."

"I judge *you* to be a wise man, my old friend."

"Well, I don't know about that, but Darius, it appears, might agree with you. He's chosen to set one hundred and twenty satraps over all of Babylonia to manage the affairs of the region. Like the royal attendants and guard, he's retained much of the old structure, but there are a few of his own people in the mix as well. As for me, he's asked me to serve with two others as high officiants over the one hundred and twenty."

"Daniel!" I exclaimed. "That is unbelievable. That makes you one of the most powerful men in the new empire."

"Maybe so, Meshach. Maybe so. But with power comes politics. I am an old man and not sure I have the stomach for the game much longer. But nevertheless, I am happy to serve the new king. He strikes me as an unusually kind man for a king. I am not sure I've met one like him before, and I certainly have met my share of kings in this life."

We both laughed. At the truth of his statement and at the absurdity that two old Jews could be this close to the center of world power.

A private entry in the Journal of Meshach
Seventh day of the month of Tebētum, the first year of the reign of
Cyrus the Great of Persia
539 B.C.

-34-

Treachery! Conspiracy!

I can see it with my eyes. I can hear it with my ears. Not all who rule in high places are at ease with a Jew having the power that my old friend Daniel is about to be handed by King Darius.

My position as royal court reporter has me in the palace each day. I am privy to the most sensitive of discussions. I am free to roam and listen and write. And I hear their whispers. I see the trap they are setting before it is even sprung.

Darius loves Daniel. The two have become as much friends as ruler and subject. The installed king trusts the wise old sage from Jerusalem. And that is enough for those with Babylonian blood coursing through their veins to devise a scheme to see "the problem Jew," as they call him, removed.

I see them, but they don't see me. I am a Jew as well. In their midst. But to them I am but a lowly scribe. A fly on the wall. Not even worth their time or notice. But I know what they are up to. I watched after the noon hour today as they presented their Trojan horse to Darius.

"A month of celebration, Oh King! From one moon to the next, let the whole population of the land bow and worship and show honor to the Great Darius of the Medes. May your words be inscribed by the royal court recorder himself and distributed throughout the land. And may all who refuse to bow only to you, Oh Darius, be cast into your den of hungry lions!"

They played on the ego of the new king and pulled him unknowingly into their web of deceit. I heard them laugh and make jokes about feeding violators to the Persian lions as if it would never happen. They know this king has no blood lust. He's a kind and gracious ruler and the lions themselves are nearly starved to death for lack of sacrifices. It just is not his way. But the poor king could not see the game behind the game. It is about Daniel. The whole month of celebration and worship to Darius is about Daniel. They know Daniel prays three times a day toward Jerusalem. On the palace grounds. On his upper porch. All who walk the grounds see him daily in this posture. And they know that nothing will stop him. Not even a decree from Darius.

There was nothing I could do to stop it. I wanted so badly to warn the king. To expose the plot. But I was helpless. I am, after all, only the royal court recorder. Who am I? Only a fly on the wall. And I was used as a tool in this act of treachery aimed at my old friend. I had to scribe the words as dictated by Darius himself, but the seeds were planted by the conspirators.

I am undone. I feel as though I myself penned the death sentence for my friend.

I must go and warn him.

A private entry in the Journal of Meshach
Twenty-fourth day of the month of Tebētum, the first year of the reign
of Cyrus the Great of Persia
539 B.C.

-35-

The decree was issued.

Thirty days of celebration and worship in the name of Darius alone.

Daniel, as always, walked to the balcony of his porch and bowed toward Jerusalem in prayer. He knew the eyes of treachery were upon him, but he boldly declared his allegiance to Yahweh nonetheless.

"Let them watch and then let them come," he told me.

I had tried to warn him, but to what end? I knew that Daniel would be Daniel. That's what makes him, well...Daniel.

And they came, just as he was finishing his time of sunrise prayer. They burst through the doors of his home and stormed the prayer porch.

"You've been cornered, Jew!" they shouted. "Only to Darius are we to bow. Under threat of death have you bowed to your God and so now you will pay the price."

"Go and do what you must do," he quietly said.

I am not sure what they expected but it was surely not this. They came looking for a fight and Daniel would not give it to them. Not even a plea for mercy. Just a quiet resignation to whatever the fates might allow. The pack of accusers turned and shuffled away.

But that did not dissuade them from carrying out their conspiracy of murder. I was there later this morning when they came before the king.

"Oh great Darius!" they shouted upon entry to the throne room. "Did you not say that to you alone are we to bow? For thirty days? But the Jew Daniel has mocked your decree. On this, the first day of celebration, he has bowed before his own God in direct opposition to your decree. He dishonors you personally, Oh King."

The king looked puzzled. He was clearly not expecting the commotion in front of him to begin his day. "Daniel?" was all he muttered.

The leader of the group continued - a foul soul of a man named Avack. "Did you not declare by law, Oh King, that anyone found not bowing to you alone should be fed to the lions? The Law of the Medes and the Persians is set and cannot be revoked."

And there it was. The noose had been placed around Daniel's neck and pulled tight. These Babylonian traitors had leaned on the legal system of Persia. They were using it against Daniel, *and Darius*, and to their own gain. The Persians are known for the strict adherence to their laws, even when the law is turned back upon itself.

I saw Darius' shoulders sag. He and Daniel are friends of sorts. As much as a king can be the friend of a subject. He treasures the old sage from Jerusalem. They have a bond. For a moment I thought this would save my old friend. I thought Darius would declare a pardon. He surely understood the schemes of those in front of him. He knew now what I had seen from its inception, that this whole idea of a month-long celebration in honor of Darius was never about Darius. It was always about Daniel. The king had been played. I knew it. They knew it. And now Darius knew it.

"Give me the day to consider Daniel's fate," he muttered to the pack of accusers.

"But the Law of the Medes and the Persians," Avack countered. "It is set. It cannot be - "

"I know my own law!" Darius thundered. "Away from me. All of you. I am sick of your sight. I will consider what can be done."

"But you must - "

"AWAY!"

And they fled. All of them. But I stayed close. It was my job. To record these events and to place them into the historical record of Persia. I sidled some distance from the king for the remainder of the day. I prayed to Yahweh that Darius would find a way, some loophole in the law that would save Daniel.

The king skipped lunch, something very unusual for him. He called for his legal counsel to attend him. There were discussions that lasted all through the afternoon. Darius excused himself every hour or so to go and check the position of the sun. He knew that Daniel's fate would be sealed by sunset if he could not find a solution.

I have served many kings in my life, but never have I seen a king carry a burden so visibly as Darius carried the fate of Daniel on his shoulders. It puzzled me. I knew he favored old Daniel, but this was extraordinary. It would be so easy for a king to simply let it go. He was a king after all, and what were mere citizens to most kings? But Darius was clearly not most kings.

The sun finally set.

Darius called for the royal guard and gave them instructions. "Be gentle with him," he ordered. "He is an old man and deserves more than the law will allow."

I rushed away as the guard made preparations. I found Daniel, in his home, finishing his sunset prayers.

"I was hoping you wouldn't be here," I said. "I was hoping you would have fled. I think Darius is hoping the same thing."

He smiled through his beard. "And where would I go, Meshach? These legs are in no shape to carry me far."

I began to weep. "Oh, Daniel. It is not right. That it should come to this. You know what these lions can do. Will do." I collapsed at his feet.

"Rise, my young friend." He placed his hand on my shoulder. "Come sit with me in these last moments. You are of more use to me at my side than at my feet."

"What will you do?" I asked as I sat next to him on a bench. It was a stunning sunset and the horizon was lit like fire from its rays.

"I think I will *do* nothing," he began. "They will come and I will go."

"But the lions..." I croaked.

"Don't worry about the lions, Meshach," he chuckled. "There is no meat on these skinny bones for hungry lions. I doubt they will find much interest in me."

"How can you joke at a time like this?"

"I am not joking, Meshach." His voice took on a stern tone and he looked at me with a fierceness I had not seen in a long, long time. "What is the mouth of a lion compared to the hand of God?" He let the question linger. "Answer me, Meshach."

"It is..."

"Say it."

"Nothing."

His smile returned. "It is nothing." He pointed with a bony finger toward the horizon. "The sky tonight reminds me of a fire that burned many years ago. I think you might remember that same fire. It was in a furnace on the Plain of Dura. Do you remember that fire, Meshach? I know it was a long time ago now, but surely you still remember."

"Yes, I remember. I can never forget."

"But you sound like a man who has already forgotten. I

was not there that day. I was away on the business of the king, but I heard the story. I even read your written account. You are very good with words, my young friend. You looked at Nebuchadnezzar and declared that you would not, that you could not, bow to him, even if that meant the fires of the furnace. And then you said something that was most remarkable. You said that God was able to deliver you. But if not... those were the magic words, Meshach. *But if not*, you still would worship only Yahweh. What is the fire of a furnace compared to the hand of God? Nothing. It is a good lesson. One I think I will cling to in this hour. God will take care of me, Meshach. But if not, all will still be well."

They came shortly after Daniel uttered those words: *But if not, all will still be well.*

They were gentle, just as Darius had ordered. I followed as we walked to the pit of lions. The accusers of Daniel were there waiting. Daniel said no words. He offered no resistance. I expected there would be shouting and accusations of treason, but Daniel's lack of fight seemed to suck the energy out of the space around the lion's den. Or maybe it was the sight of a skinny old man being led by guards to his death. How was this man any threat to anyone? The absurdity of the moment was palpable.

The guards fastened a harness around Daniel's buttocks and midsection. He moved to sit on the stone wall built around the massive hole in the ground that led to the stomachs of the beasts waiting for him.

Daniel's gaze looked past me and past his accusers and fixated on something in the distance. I turned my head to see what it was. No! Not something. Someone. It was King Darius. He had come but could not bring himself to come too close.

"Daniel!" he called out. "May your God, whom you serve continually, deliver you!"

It was a stunning moment. A king appealing to a God he did not know to deliver Daniel from a fate that he himself had ordered.

And then Daniel smiled. Yes, Daniel smiled. Like always.

I watched as he was lowered into the lion's den. I watched until I could see his smile no longer. I watched as a stone was rolled over the top of the hole. I watched as the king's seal was placed on the stone.

And then I closed my eyes.

With eyes closed I could see Daniel's smile once again.

And I heard his final words to me. *God will take care of me, Meshach. But if not, all will still be well.*

A private entry in the Journal of Meshach
Twenty-fifth day of the month of Tebētum, the first year of the reign of
Cyrus the Great of Persia
539 B.C.

-36-

I spent the night at the den of lions.

A guard was posted to keep away any who might attempt a rescue. They had nothing to fear from me. I am too old and weak to move a stone and pull a man out of a hole in the ground. But I am not too old to pray. So that is what I did. I prayed and prayed till the dawn sun broke the sky.

Just as the day began to break, I heard a rustling of feet on dirt and witnessed a frantic King Darius rushing to the pit. He had clearly not slept either. Once again, this new king surprises me. Why does he care this much about an aged Jew?

"Move it!" he commanded. "Move the stone now."

The soldiers hastened to the task. The seal was broken and the stone was cast aside.

There was a hush among the small gathered crowd.

Darius inched his way toward the mouth of the den. His voice carried with it a tone of anguish as he called out, "Daniel! Can you hear me? Are you alive? Has your God done the impossible? Has he saved you?"

And then there was quiet. The moment dragged on for what seemed an eternity. I found myself shuffling toward the opening of the pit myself, daring to hope but not wanting to see inside something that would vanquish my hope.

I startled back as a roar came bellowing from the mouth of the den. But it was not the roar of a lion. It was the roar of a man!

"Long live the king!"

It was Daniel! He was alive. The impossible had become possible.

Daniel called out again, "My God sent his angel to shut the lions' mouths so that they would not hurt me, for I have been found innocent in his sight. God did not allow the lions to harm me, because he knows that I never harmed you, Oh King!"

King Darius clasped his hands together in praise and fell to his knees. He looked into the pit as if to verify that Daniel was indeed alive and safe. I rushed to the pit myself. It was an amazing sight. Daniel was relaxed, sitting on the floor of the pit with his back against the rock wall. Three lions lounged opposite my old friend, seemingly uninterested in the Jew from Jerusalem. They acted, in fact, as if he wasn't even there.

"Quick, out with him!" Darius ordered.

The guard went to work, lowering the rope and harness. It was but a moment later that that face I love crested the rim of the stone wall around the pit. And yes, it was smiling.

Once he'd been fully extracted from the lions' den, Darius made one more remarkable move. He embraced old Daniel.

I've decided I like this king.

Pulling away, Darius' demeanor changed. "I want the accusers of this man brought at once to the pit. Bring their families too and throw the lot of them to the lions. Let's see if the god they worship will find them innocent and save them in the manner that Daniel's God has saved him. I doubt such will be the case."

It was a stunning move. While Darius is kindhearted, it is clear he also has a spine of iron and will not tolerate treachery and conspiracy in his court.

"Meshach!" I jumped as he called my name. "Come with me. I need you to write something for me."

I had no time to rejoice with Daniel as we hurried away. I will plan to eat dinner with him this evening and have him tell me the whole story about this angel that came to his rescue. But first I followed the king to his workroom.

"Meshach, get your parchment and quill and write what I say, and then see that it is posted to all people of all tongues throughout the empire."

I obeyed and then King Darius began to dictate:

Peace be multiplied to you. I make a decree, that in all my royal dominion people are to tremble and fear before the God of Daniel, for he is the living God, enduring forever; his kingdom shall never be destroyed, and his dominion shall be to the end. He delivers and rescues; he works signs and wonders in heaven and on earth, he who has saved Daniel from the power of the lions.

I wrote and then I ordered the royal scribes to make copies and then I ordered the royal couriers to carry the message to the stretches of the Persian Empire. Just as King Darius ordered.

Yes, I like this king, indeed.

A private entry in the Journal of Meshach

Twenty-sixth day of the month of Tebētum, the first year of the reign of Cyrus the Great of Persia
539 B.C.

-37-

My friend, Daniel, died today.

I was there by his side as he breathed his last breath and was gathered to our fathers. He was eighty-five years old. I stayed with his body until those that are to prepare it for burial came. King Darius has ordered a day of mourning throughout the empire, and a royal procession to a tomb in the district of the kings. It is the highest honor that can be bestowed on any citizen not of royal birth in all the Persian Empire.

As one final act of service to my friend, I will oversee all these matters until the last stone is laid in place covering his tomb.

I was blessed with one final conversation with old Daniel early this morning before he passed from this world to the next.

"How will I manage alone in this world without you by my side, old friend?" I asked him as he lay on his bed.

"I think you will manage quite fine once I am out of the way," he chuckled through a cough.

"How can you joke about something like death?" I chided him. "I'm serious Daniel. I've known you my whole life it seems. Longer than any other soul I've ever encountered. I will miss you dearly."

"And I will miss you, my young friend." His bony, wrinkled hand reached up and clasped my own bony wrinkled hand. "But I suspect we will be together again. Sooner rather than later." He squeezed out another snicker.

I was somber. "Yes, I think you are correct."

"We have seen much in this life, Meshach. You and I. Our greatest curse – being ripped from our home and our families – turned in to our greatest blessing. We have traveled the world. We have sat in the court of kings, both good and bad. We have watched from the front row as the gods have warred with one another, and we've seen Yahweh victorious every time. We have witnessed firsthand the evil that men can do to other men. And we've seen how God can redeem the most vile of men and make him a servant of the Most High. You, my friend, have walked through fire, and I have slept with the lions. We've seen and done more than most ever will. We have lived blessed lives."

I squeezed his hand and then set it down over his chest. The time of passing was growing close. I could sense it. "You know, Daniel. I used to be angry at God. Angry that he took me from my family. Angry that he took me from Jerusalem. I had plans and dreams for my life. I would follow in my father's footsteps and serve as counsel for the king of Judah. I would live in the shadow of the Holy Temple in Jerusalem and worship Yahweh with the weekly and annual sacrifices. I would marry in Jerusalem and raise my children in Jerusalem. And then I would die in Jerusalem. Those were my plans."

I paused to check on Daniel. I did not want to miss the holy moment.

"Yes," he said. "Go on. I am still here. You have more to say, I know."

This time I was the one that smiled. "But God had other plans for my life. You know, as I think about it, I think this is how God must work with all people to one degree or another. We have dreams and plans of life in Jerusalem. But then God takes us to Babylon. I never wanted to go to Babylon, Daniel. I hated Babylon. Babylon was the Black

Wind. But Babylon is where I went. Not by choice, but by force. But it was in Babylon that I discovered God in a new way. I learned more about God in Babylon than I ever would have learned if I had stayed in Jerusalem. And you are right. I have seen more sights and lived more life than I deserve...all because I embraced the life God gave me instead of growing bitter and wishing for a life that was more my idea than his."

Daniel smiled at me one more time. He was too weak to say anymore in reply.

A tear leaked from my eye and traveled down my face before being swallowed by my gray beard. "So, yes, my old friend," I whispered in his ear. "We have both lived and now it is time to die. It is okay. I will be fine. You can go now. And you are right...I will not be far behind."

And then he was gone.

My friend, Daniel, died today.

A private entry in the Journal of Meshach
Third day of the month of Abu, the fourth year of the reign of Cyrus the Great of Persia
536 B.C.

A Word Before We End...

And that, dear reader, is my story.

My life.

Thank you for taking a portion of your life to read about mine. Like my old friend, Daniel, I am nearly done. It is time for me to go.

As I think back on my life, what I see more than anything else are the faces. Yes, there are memories of both good times and bad times. Memories of pain and memories of joy. But more than all of those combined are the faces.

The face of my father.

The face of my mother.

The face of Ruth, my sister.

The face of Mary, my wife.

The face of my two beloved friends: Shadrach and Abednego.

The face of my best friend, Daniel.

All of these faces have gone on ahead of me. I am the last one left.

Very soon I will close these eyes for the last time. Perhaps it will be tonight. I wouldn't mind. But if not, it will not be long. And when I close these eyes for the last time, I know that when they open...on the other side...I will see those faces again. Not as a memory. No. But face to face! But there will be one face I will rush to find. I only saw this face one time in my life and it was oh, so brief. It was more than most men ever get in this life and enough to leave me wanting more. To see that face again. And not a glimpse, but full on.

I want to see that face. I long to see that face. The face of the one who stood with me in the fires of the furnace. The face of the one who placed his hand on my shoulder.

The face of the one who saved me.

That is the face I look forward to seeing the most.

And so now, dear reader, the time has come. There is no more for me to write. I lay aside my quill and I put away my parchment.

I am not a king and I am not a god. I am like most men on earth. Simple. Ordinary. Forgettable.

My name is Meshach.

AFTERWARD

I never planned to write this book. I am currently in the middle of a multi-volume work of fiction involving the adventures of a college professor named Dr. Phineas T. Crook who continually finds himself in the midst of trouble and has a knack for pulling his friends along for the ride.

While writing the second volume of the series, *The King's Disease*, I chose to use the literary device of an ancient journal to transition the four parts of the book and to hint of what was to come. That ancient journal was *The Journal of Meshach* (but only four short entries).

Somewhere along the way I began to wonder...what if? A dangerous thing for writers to do. And so, I couldn't resist. The moment I was done writing *The King's Disease*, I dove right in to fleshing out a full *Journal of Meshach*. The source material, the biblical book of Daniel, was dripping with fruit to be picked. The temptation became too much to say no to. And so, I hope you enjoyed this impromptu labor of love.

Further inspiration for this type of biblical historical fiction comes from my love for the great Gene Edwards. From the moment I read *The Divine Romance*, followed quickly by *A Tale of Three Kings*, and then *The Prisoner in the Third Cell*, I was an admirer of how Gene crafted the biblical text into riveting stories that poignantly "read between the lines." Thank you, Gene Edwards, for the inspiration to take my own stab at this type of literature.

Thanks also to my wife, Julie, who faithfully endures my crazy ideas involving fiction and walks right alongside me, reading, and re-reading, and reading yet again the manuscripts in their various forms, offering advice and applying her considerable editorial skill.

Gayla Oldham and Jill Langham, it is a joy to work with you both daily in our office at Cross Church. I am thankful for your encouragement of my work and for reading and assisting in the very laborious process of editing. Books are a group effort, and this one is no exception

ABOUT THE AUTHOR

Jeffrey S. Crawford is teaching pastor and lead pastor of ministries at Cross Church in northwest Arkansas, one of the largest and fastest growing megachurches in North America. He holds a Doctorate of Education in Leadership from the Southern Baptist Theological Seminary, a Master of Divinity degree from Southwestern Baptist Theological Seminary, and a Bachelor of Arts in Philosophy from Oklahoma Baptist University. He has served for over thirty years in churches across Arkansas, Texas, Oklahoma, Louisiana, Utah, and Tennessee and enjoys traveling the globe on missionary journeys and interacting with the peoples of the world. He and his wife, Julie, have raised their four children in the foothills of the Ozarks where they make their home.

Made in the USA
Monee, IL
18 September 2021